QUICK CASH IN FORECLOSURES

QUICK CASH IN FORECLOSURES

Chantal Howell Carey and Bill Carey

John Wiley & Sons, Inc.

This book is printed on acid-free paper. ♾

Published by John Wiley & Sons, Inc., Hoboken, New Jersey

Published simultaneously in Canada

Disclaimer: Every stated "we" was not necessarily the writers' but could be the writers' clients or students. "We" is used to protect the privacy of those concerned.

For general information on our other products and services, or technical support, please contact our Customer Care Department within the United States at (800) 762-2974, outside the United States at (317) 572-3993 or fax (317) 572-4002.

Wiley also publishes its books in a variety of electronic formats. Some content that appears in print may not be available in electronic books. For more information about Wiley products, visit our web site at www.wiley.com.

Library of Congress Cataloging-in-Publication Data:

Howell-Carey, Chantal.
Quick cash in foreclosures / Chantal Howell Carey and Bill Carey.
p. cm.
Includes index.
ISBN 0-471-67955-0 (pbk.)
1. Real estate investment—United States. 2. Foreclosure—United States. 3. House buying—United States. 4. Real property—Purchasing—United States. I. Carey, Bill, 1951- II. Title.

HD255.H663 2004
332.63'243—dc22 2004042251

Printed in the United States of America.
10 9 8 7 6 5 4 3 2

CONTENTS

PREFACE

The national foreclosure rate has increased dramatically over the last four years. Today more than 2 out of every 100 mortgage loans are in the foreclosure process. The numbers according to the Mortgage Bankers Association say that 500,000 to 600,000 mortgages are either delinquent or in foreclosure. In the Dallas area foreclosures have increased 85 percent since 1999. With the recession of 2001 and the jobless recovery, 3 million people have lost their jobs. They continue to fall behind in their mortgage payments.

We feel one of the best opportunities of the last 25 years to make money investing in foreclosures is about to occur. Over the next three years people who invest in real estate foreclosures are going to make tens of thousands of dollars. This book from our Win Going In! series, *Quick Cash in Foreclosures,* is designed to introduce both the new and the seasoned real estate investor to a new way to make money in the foreclosure market.

Using the techniques we developed in our book *The New Path to Real Estate Wealth: Earning Without Owning* (2004), we show you how to flip your foreclosure deals for Quick Cash. Unlike any of the other foreclosure books on the market, this book presents a way to make money in foreclosures without having a lot of cash to invest.

The most expensive way to invest in foreclosures is buying them at the foreclosure sale. In April 2004 we went to the foreclosure sale on the steps of the Tarrant County courthouse in Fort Worth, Texas. There were more than one thousand properties being auctioned to the highest bidder. There were almost five hundred people milling around trying to figure out how to bid. You had a 500 to 1 shot of getting one of the top deals. And because of the competition, your final *cash* price was going to be bid up past the point of making any profit on the deal. Needless to say, we didn't bid on any properties that day.

The key to *Quick Cash in Foreclosures* is successfully negotiating with the seller in pre-foreclosure. We show you how to buy the seller's equity for pennies on the dollar. Once you have negotiated a wholesale contract with the seller, we teach you how to flip, assign, or option your contract to another investor for a fat fee before the property goes to the foreclosure sale. You make Quick Cash with no cash out of your pocket, no qualifying for a loan, no battling the hordes on the courthouse steps, no fix-up costs, no carrying costs, and no resale costs.

Quick Cash in Foreclosures is the only foreclosure book that shows you how to start with little or no knowledge of the foreclosure process and little or no money, and make Quick Cash in the foreclosure game. When we developed and produced the foreclosure training for Robert Allen, author of the best seller *Nothing Down,* our students in Baltimore and Los Angeles were able to put into practice the insider knowledge we presented to make money investing in foreclosures immediately. With this book, you will be able to do what our students did from coast to coast!

INTRODUCTION

Over the years we have traveled throughout the country teaching real estate, financial, motivational, and interpersonal skills seminars to our students. We are always striving to be on the leading edge.

Regarding real estate, we have taught everything from buying and selling it creatively as an individual or investor to core classes for licensing and passing real estate broker's exams. Just about anything you can think of related to real estate, we have taught to someone somewhere!

With a new millennium comes new ideas. We have distilled the knowledge and experience we have gained from buying and selling real estate for ourselves and our clients and helping our students over the last three decades.

Quick Cash in Foreclosures is the seventh real estate book we have written. Our first book, *How to Sell Your Home Without a Broker,* is in its fourth edition (2004). The third edition of that book was picked as one of the top 10 real estate books for 2001 by Robert J. Bruss in the *Los Angeles Times.*

Our fourth book, *Going Going Gone! Auctioning Your Home for Top Dollar,* was also written to benefit the homeowner in the selling of a home. Like *How to Sell Your Home Without a Broker,* our auctioning book was designed to show you how to successfully sell your home yourself without paying a real estate commission.

Our fifth book, *The New Path to Real Estate Wealth: Earning Without Owning,* was the first book in our new series designed specifically for real estate investors. This Win Going In! series is designed to take you from being a novice real estate investor to an expert.

Our premise for the Win Going In! series is that no matter what kind of real estate investment you are going to make, you have to win going in. It is no longer enough to make money on the back end of a deal or make a profit when you get out of a deal. The deal has to have a profit built in on the front end, or else you shouldn't do it at all.

Quick Cash in Foreclosures is the second book in the Win Going In! series. We show you here how to make money going into a foreclosure deal. This is a hands-on book that teaches you how to enter the real estate foreclosure market and make deals happen. What is unique about this book is that we show you how to have a Quick Cash investment strategy that you can successfully implement with little or no investment capital.

We recommend you read this book in a particular way. Bring a lot of energy to your reading. This doesn't mean that you have to necessarily read the book quickly, though that is fine with us. We want you to be excited about the material. We want you to win going in as you read.

If you find yourself bogging down, stop reading. The material is designed to be comprehended in bursts. See if you can go from one light bulb turning on in your mind to the next. As it gets brighter and brighter you will find yourself energized.

Our purpose for the Win Going In! series is to teach you all our real estate knowledge and expertise. We want to be the Brain Trust for your successful real estate investment career. You will know you are a successful investor when you make money on your first deal.

We would love to hear from you about your successes. Also, we want to hear what is working and what is not working for you. Please e-mail us at thetrustee@hotmail.com or contact us through our publisher, John Wiley & Sons. Good luck and good deals!

Chantal & Bill Carey

QUICK CASH IN FORECLOSURES

CHAPTER 1

Quick Cash in Foreclosures

Some real estate investors employ the real estate investment strategy of *long-term wealth building.* In long-term wealth building you buy and hold property for income and appreciation. This can be a very effective strategy in areas of the country that experience very high rates of price appreciation, such as California and the Northeast.

However, once you invest your money in real estate, it can be difficult to liquidate or sell your assets quickly. Because real estate is the biggest ticket item there is, it has the fewest buyers in the marketplace compared with any other commodity. The *Quick Cash* strategy addresses the problem historically associated with real estate investing: the lack of liquidity.

Quick Cash Strategy

We recommend you use a Quick Cash strategy to make money in foreclosures. Another name for the Quick Cash strategy is *flipping*. Flipping is the fastest way to make money in real estate. When you flip a property, you get in and out of a property in a short period of time.

Investing in foreclosures can be very cash-intensive. When you buy a foreclosure on the courthouse steps, you have to pay cash. There usually are fix-up expenses with foreclosures that require cash outlays. There may be carrying costs, like mortgage payments, property taxes, and homeowner association fees. You may have to flip your foreclosure property so you can get your cash out and be able to go in on another foreclosure deal.

Top 10 Advantages of the Quick Cash Strategy

We are going to give you the top 10 advantages when you use the Quick Cash strategy. The Quick Cash strategy is especially useful for foreclosure investing. We like Quick Cash—a.k.a. flipping—because we don't like landlording (we've tried it), we love the art of the deal (flipping allows you to make lots of deals), and we like making money right away.

Number 10: No Income Tax Problems

One of the major advantages of the Quick Cash strategy is that you avoid income tax problems. When you hold rental real estate, it is very easy to recapture depreciation when you sell the property. Currently, if you have recapture of depreciation, you pay 25 percent in taxes. How easy is it to recapture depreciation? Just own rental real estate and take depreciation.

Number 9: No Extensive Record Keeping

Can you say "certified public accountant" (CPA)? When you own rental real estate, you must keep extensive records. You will have a full-time job as a CPA, or you will be paying a CPA.

You will have rent receipts. Security deposit receipts. Checkbooks (notice we use the plural here). You will have checking accounts to reconcile. How about the legal requirement in some areas of having a trust account for tenant security deposits?

You will keep maintenance records. You may have employees with all the paperwork and tax nightmares that entails. Workers' compensation insurance, unemployment insurance, health insurance, OSHA (Occupational Safety and Hazards Association), Social Security taxes, withholding federal income taxes. The list goes on.

Number 8: No Lawsuits

If you own real property, there is a high probability that you will be sued—if not by one of your tenants or guests, then by a cutthroat attorney who looks up your real estate holdings in the public record to determine if they will take a case based on the real estate assets you own that they can go after.

When you own property, you are a target for frivolous lawsuits. Some of you reading this already know exactly what we are talking about. You have been sued for no apparent reason. We also know that some of you have paid legal settlements just to make the frivolous lawsuits go away.

Our solution? Don't own real property. Not even foreclosure property. Control real property. How do you control real property and not own real property? Good question. That is what the Quick Cash strategy is all about!

Number 7: No Homeowner Association

If you are, or have ever been, part of a homeowner association, then you know the frustration of dealing with minityrants. Not to mention the $100, $200, or $300 monthly dues. Or special assessments for painting, landscaping, or roofing that can run into the thousands of dollars. And if you don't pay your monthly dues or special assessments, then your friendly homeowner association can foreclose on you and/or sue you.

Homeowner associations are no longer just attached to condominiums or townhouses. We are seeing more and more "maintenance associations" attached to planned unit developments (PUDs) and single-family residences (houses).

Number 6: No Repairs and Maintenance Costs

We are sure you have heard the expression "deferred maintenance." Deferred maintenance is the polite way of saying a property is a fixer-upper because the property owner spent no money on regular maintenance through the years. When a property is in foreclosure, you can bet the last thing the property owner is going to spend money on is repairs and maintenance.

New roof: $7,500. New dishwasher: $400. Gardener: $100 monthly. Pool maintenance: $75 monthly. Real estate ownership entails significant repairs and maintenance costs. Flipping property helps you avoid these costs.

Number 5: No Hazard Insurance

No fire insurance, no liability insurance, no earthquake insurance. No insurance, period. The last time we checked, any kind of hazard insurance is expensive. And real estate lenders calculate a monthly insurance payment when qualifying you for a real estate loan, even when you prepay the insurance premium in an escrow account for the next year.

Number 4: No Property Taxes

Depending on your state, you may pay property taxes once or perhaps twice a year. In states like Texas, where there is no state income tax, property taxes can be quite substantial on even modest properties.

On a property valued at $137,000 by the county tax assessor in our area near Fort Worth, the annual property tax bill can amount to $4,000! If you calculate that on a monthly basis, you are paying $333 a month for every month you own the property.

Monthly Property Taxes

Annual Property Taxes	$4,000
Monthly Property Taxes	$ 333

Number 3: No Monthly Mortgage Payments

Month in and month out, 12 months a year for 30 years: 360 payments. Let's look at an example. A $200,000 loan for 30 years at 8 percent interest is payable at $1,467.53 monthly, including principal and interest. Multiply the monthly payment by 360 payments, and you will pay a total of $528,310.80.

Monthly Payments

Monthly Payment	$ 1,467.53
30 Years	× 360
Total Payments	$528,310.80

The really nauseating number is when you realize that you originally borrowed $200,000! You wind up paying $328,310.80 in interest. That is 164 percent of the amount you borrowed.

Amount of Interest

Total Payments	$528,310.80
Amount Borrowed	$200,000.00
Amount of Interest	$329,310.80

Number 2: No Landlording

Do we really have to tell you our landlording horror stories? Do you really think you can be a successful landlord? Being a landlord is a heartless, thankless job. No matter what you do, you are wrong. Okay, okay, we will tell you one of our landlording horror stories.

Landlording Horror Story Being a lord or lady of the land has a noble heritage. In olden times there was a symbiotic relationship between the lords and ladies and their tenants. The tenants lived on the lords' and ladies' property, raised their families, and farmed the land.

In return the tenants paid rent to the lords and ladies in the form of most of the crops they grew. There was no money. Or, at least, most people, like the tenants, did not have money because there were no jobs. Everyone's "job" was working the land.

Unfortunately, this romantic symbiotic relationship from the Middle Ages has been shattered by the realities of today's world. As a landlord you are a target for other people's problems. And as a target you become the recipient of a lot of crap. On to our horror story. We have so many. Concrete in the toilet. Concrete in the kitchen sink. Concrete in the oven. Which one would you like to hear? On second thought, we think we will pass. Too many bad memories. Bottom line: We recommend you avoid landlording.

Number 1: Quick Cash

And the number 1 advantage of the Quick Cash strategy is Quick Cash. Cash is king! Long live the king! The problem with real estate investing for most people is that it takes far too long to make any money. Yes, we know that if you bought a two-bedroom, one-bathroom home in Coronado, California, in 1968 for $20,000, like our friend John did, you would be sitting on a property worth $900,000 today. But who has the time, or the patience, to wait? We don't; do you?

Flipping is your answer. When you are a real estate investor whose strategy is Quick Cash, patience does not have to be one of your strengths. In fact, being impatient becomes one of your strengths! You become impatient with the deal you are working on and want to get it done so you can get on to the next deal. The more foreclosure deals you get involved with, the more money you will make.

Flipping-First Attitude

We will give you several examples so you can get a sense of the many opportunities that flipping provides to make Quick Cash. By studying the examples, we hope you will start to expand the way you look at buying and selling real estate. When you have a flipping-first attitude, you will discover new ways to make money in real estate unforeseen by the average real estate investor.

When you apply a flipping-first attitude to the foreclosure market, you will have a competitive advantage over other foreclosure investors. Rather than just buying foreclosures on the courthouse steps, we will show you how to buy foreclosures in the pre-foreclosure stage directly from the seller. We will also show you how to tie up a foreclosure property with a contract that you can flip to another real estate investor. But first things first.

There are two main tactics in the flipping strategy. The first is what we call Find and Flip. You find a property knowing that you are going to flip it as soon as you can. You may close escrow on the property before you flip it. Or, you may flip the property even before you own it! The second tactic is what we call Find, Fix, and Flip. You find a property, you do the fix up as quickly as possible, and then you flip the property.

Find and Flip

Example 1 We found a seller who wanted to get out of his rental properties. We made an offer on a 600-square-foot studio efficiency condo in Del Mar, California. The property was tenant occupied and rented for

$700 a month. It was located one freeway exit away from the location of the annual Del Mar Summer Fair and Del Mar Thoroughbred Race Track, where the "Turf Meets the Surf." The tenant was planning on staying.

The seller sold us the condo for $63,000, which was the loan amount to the bank. The value of the condo was $72,000. The seller basically signed over the deed and walked away from the property. We made no down payment. We took over the existing $63,000 bank loan. Why would a seller do this?

As real estate investors, we must allow sellers to make up their own minds. While we might never, ever accept that same offer if we were the seller, we cannot presume to know the seller's motivation or ultimate goal.

Potential Profit

Value of Condo	$72,000
Purchase Price	$63,000
Potential Profit	$ 9,000

How did we make money in this deal? We found another real estate investor who wanted rental income property. The real estate investor gave us $4,000 cash, and we gave him the title to the property in the form of a quitclaim deed. We "owned" the property one week! By flipping the property, we had an immediate $4,000 profit and no landlording headaches.

Our Profit

Sales Price	$67,000
Purchase Price	$63,000
Our Profit	$ 4,000

Example 2 We found a piece of vacant land that was worth $1 million. We discovered the seller was motivated to sell. The seller wanted his price but was flexible on terms. We have found a fundamental truth in the real estate investing marketplace. *If the seller wants their price, you get your terms.* We have found the corollary to be true, too. *If the seller wants their terms* (like all cash for their equity), *you get your price.*

We offered the seller $1 million for the property. Did we have $1 million? *No!* How much down payment did we have? *Zero.* How much of a bank loan did we want to get? *Zero.* Who was going to be the lender? *The seller!*

How much was the seller willing to "loan" us? $1 million. For how long was the seller willing to loan us the $1 million? *Five years.* What was the monthly loan payment we wanted to make? *Zero.* What was the interest rate the seller would accept? *6 percent.* How was the interest to be paid? *Annually.*

Let us summarize. We offered the seller $1 million for his piece of land. We made no down payment and had no monthly payments. We would owe the seller $60,000 annually (6 percent of the $1 million "loan").

Purchase Price

Purchase Price	$1,000,000
Down Payment	0
Loan Amount	$1,000,000

Did we want to pay the seller $60,000 in 12 months? *No!* Did we have any money in this deal? *No.* How did we make money on this deal? We flipped the property! We turned around and sold the property to a new buyer within 30 days after closing.

How much did we flip the property for? We flipped the property for $1 million. How much down payment did we get? We accepted zero down payment! Did we ask the new buyer to get a loan from a bank? No. How much did we "loan" the buyer? $1 million.

For how long did we loan the buyer $1 million? Five years. Did we get monthly payments on our $1 million loan? No. What was the interest rate we negotiated? 8 percent. How was the interest to be paid? Annually.

Resale Price

Sales Price	$1,000,000
Down Payment	0
Loan Amount	$1,000,000

The buyer would owe us $80,000 annually (8 percent of the $1 million "loan"). Do you see how we made money? When we received our $80,000 payment, we paid our $60,000 payment, leaving us $20,000 profit! The fact that we had to wait 12 months to make our money was fine with us. It worked out to be $1,666.67 per month!

Our Profit

Money Received	$80,000
Money Paid Out	$60,000
Our Profit	$20,000

Find, Fix, and Flip

Example 3 We found a property that was a three-bedroom, two-bath, 1,900-square-foot, single-family residence in a good neighborhood. The owners were in the process of getting a divorce. They had moved out of the property in anticipation of foreclosure.

The property was a mess. The roof needed repair. The carpets had to be replaced. The floor coverings were beyond repair. Painting was needed inside and out. The landscaping was early jungle. The pool was a breeding ground for West Nile virus–carrying mosquitoes.

We got the sellers' written permission to talk to their lender. We were able to delay the foreclosure for 60 days. We wrote an offer for 65 percent of what we determined to be the retail value of the property. The retail value is the value a property has for an end user like a homeowner.

We felt the retail value was $135,000. Our offer was for $84,500, all cash, at closing. The offer was also contingent on our money partner's approval. If our money partner didn't approve of the deal, we had no deal. The sellers accepted our offer with no counteroffer.

Potential Profit

Value of House	$135,000
Purchase Price	$ 84,500
Potential Profit	$ 50,500

We brought in our clean-up crew and in five days had stripped out the carpeting and floor coverings, cut back the jungle landscaping, drained and cleaned the pool, and painted the entire interior of the house Navaho white. We did nothing about the roof. Our total cost was $2,200. We left the big stuff for the next real estate investor.

We started calling down our list of real estate investors who liked to do major fix up. The third real estate investor we showed the property to wanted to buy it. We had the purchase price of $84,500 plus our fix-up cost of $2,200 in the property, for a total of $86,700. We sold the property for $92,500 10 days after we had made our offer to the seller. We got our fix-up cost back plus made $5,800. Not bad for 10 days' work.

Our Profit

Sales Price	$92,500
Purchase Price	$84,500
Fix Up	$ 2,200
Our Profit	$ 5,800

Example 4 Sometimes a real estate deal gets you more involved in the fix-up phase than you want to be. This can especially be the case with foreclosure property. This example is instructive in two ways. First, it is another example of Find, Fix, and Flip. Second, it is an example of getting too involved with the fix-up phase.

We found a property that was headed into foreclosure. It was a four-bedroom, three-bath, 2,700-square-foot, single-family home in a good neighborhood. The property was vacant. Again, we wrote our offer for 65 percent of the retail value. We felt the retail value was $200,000. Our offer was for $130,000, cash.

Potential Profit

Value of House	$200,000
Purchase Price	$130,000
Potential Profit	$ 70,000

We felt we were getting a great deal. We thought we would spend $20,000 on the fix up and sell the property for at least $190,000 to $195,000. We would get our $20,000 fix-up money back plus make at least $40,000. Unfortunately for us, that is not the way the deal turned out.

Our $20,000 fix-up budget blew up in our faces. Once we started tearing the house up, we found mold and dry rot. This was not good. We wound up spending closer to $30,000. Still, we felt we would be all right. We would just make less profit.

At this point in our real estate investing, we were doing the major fix up. We would buy the property and do all the fix up. Then we would sell the property to a retail buyer homeowner. We felt this was the way to go because it was how we would make the most money.

With this property we had gotten into major remodeling. It was the biggest fix up we had ever done. We realized too late that we were no longer real estate investors on this property; rather, we were in the remodeling business. Instead of doing the remodeling for a homeowner who was going to pay us, we were the homeowner!

We had another problem with this property. We had one of the best properties in the neighborhood. Ninety-eight percent of the properties in the neighborhood were not as nice and were priced less than the property we were trying to sell.

We first tried to sell the property for $200,000. No offers in 30 days. We lowered the price to $190,000. No offers in two weeks. We lowered the price to $180,000. Again, no offers in two weeks. We were starting to get nervous.

It had taken us 60 days to fix up the property. We were now another 60 days into the mission. We were making payments on the $100,000 first mortgage held by the bank. We were making payments on the $30,000 second mortgage the seller had carried back for six months. We had almost $30,000 out of our pocket in fix-up costs.

We finally sold the property, right at the six-month deadline, for $165,000. We lost money on the deal but felt fortunate that we got most of the money we had put into the property back. Right then and there we realized we never wanted to be in that position again. We knew real estate investing worked. We knew flipping worked. We decided owning and fixing property didn't work.

Our Profit

Sales Price	$165,000
Purchase Price	$130,000
Fix Up	$ 30,000
Payments	$ 6,600
Our Profit	($ 1,600)

We are now going to get into the foreclosure arena. Starting from the basics, we will show you how to apply the Quick Cash strategy to your foreclosure investing. For those of you who are knowledgeable about foreclosures, we recommend you go to chapters that grab your interest. May we suggest Chapter 14, "Flipping Foreclosures." For those of you who are new to the foreclosure game, we recommend you read straight through the book, continuing on with Chapter 2, "What Is a Foreclosure?"

CHAPTER 2

What Is a Foreclosure?

Over the next three years, when interest rates rise and the housing market cools, there are going to be many foreclosure opportunities. The economy and the real estate market are cyclical. There is a lot of money to be made in the real estate foreclosure market. But you have to be very knowledgeable about traditional foreclosures before you get involved with Quick Cash foreclosures.

Our focus is to teach you how to flip any properties you acquire in the foreclosure arena. Even better, we will show you how to flip the real estate foreclosure paperwork to another real estate investor for a fee. The Quick Cash strategy does not change just because you are dealing with foreclosures.

We are going to spend some time training you in the foreclosure process. Every state has a slightly different method on how they go through their foreclosure procedures. However, the basic process is the same in every state. What varies from state to state is the time periods allowed for foreclosure. Do not get too caught up in what may seem to be very technical information. We present this information so you can get the flavor of what is involved in a foreclosure.

Foreclosure

There is no more dreaded word in the real estate world than *foreclosure.* It doesn't matter if you are the real estate borrower or the real estate lender. No one likes to be in a foreclosure situation.

Foreclosure is when a real estate lender, whether an institutional real estate lender or a private real estate lender, takes the title to a property away from the borrower in lieu of receiving mortgage payments. Stated more formally, when all else has failed, a real estate lender will pursue allowed legal prerogatives to recover the collateral for the real estate loan in order to sell it and recoup their loan proceeds.

The definition of foreclosure is to shut out, exclude, bar, or deprive a person of the right to redeem a mortgage. Foreclosure is not only a process to recover a lender's collateral but also a procedure whereby a borrower's rights of redemption are eliminated and all interests in the subject property are removed.

Power of Sale Foreclosure

A power of sale foreclosure is based on the terms of the deed of trust or the mortgage contract, giving the lender, or the trustee, the right to sell the collateral property without being required to spend the time and money involved in a court foreclosure suit.

Texas

In Texas, for example, these nonjudical, power of sale foreclosures are more common than judical foreclosures (lawsuits in court). The right to exercise the power of sale must be created in writing and is usually part of the deed of trust, which must clearly state that there is a right of nonjudical foreclosure. The power of sale foreclosure is popular in Texas because it allows the trustee to sell the property more quickly and thus recover the lender's collateral in a timely manner.

In Texas the trustee named in the deed of trust has the power to sell the defaulted mortgaged property upon the request of the real estate lender or beneficiary of the trust deed. The trustee must then carefully follow the terms and conditions stated in the deed of trust for the foreclosure. The foreclosure sale must also follow the legal procedures of the state of Texas.

Texas Property Code

The Texas Property Code contains the following procedures for nonjudicial foreclosure. You can check what your state procedures are by contacting a real estate attorney or your local title insurance company.

1. The trustee must notify the debtor of the foreclosure sale at least 21 days before the date of the sale. This notice is to be sent by certified mail to the debtor's last known address.
2. Notice must be posted at the courthouse door of the county in which the property is located and filed in the county clerk's office where the sale is to be held.
3. The sale must be a public auction held between 10:00 A.M. and 4:00 P.M. on the first Tuesday of the month.
4. The sale must take place in the county where the property is located.
5. The holder of the debt on residential property must give the debtor at least 20 days to cure the default before the entire debt can be accelerated and declared due and the notice of sale given.

At the Foreclosure Sale

At the foreclosure sale, the trustee has an obligation to act impartially and can take no action that would discourage bidders. This is to be a public auction open to all persons, including the lender and the trustee.

There is no requirement in Texas that the auction generate fair-market value; therefore, the property will go to the highest cash bidder. The purchaser of the foreclosed property takes the title without any covenants through an instrument called a trustee's deed.

The proceeds from the sale will be used to pay the trustee and any expenses of the trustee's sale. Then the lender who is foreclosing will be paid. If there is money still left, those creditors who had filed liens against the property will be paid. Finally, any surplus monies must be returned to the borrower/debtor.

In Texas, as in every other state, if a senior lien holder forecloses, all junior lien holders' interests terminate. If a junior lien forecloses, they get the title to the property subject to the senior lien holder's interest in the property.

Judical Foreclosure and Sale

Judical foreclosure and sale is a legal procedure that involves the use of the courts and the consequent sale of the collateral. Foreclosure by court order is an alternative method that may be used in Texas and other states, although it is not favored by commercial lenders. It is the only remedy if a deed of trust does not contain a power of sale provision.

How It Works

The delinquent mortgagors are notified of the default and the reasons for it. They are also informed that an immediate solution is required and that all their efforts must be expended to solve the problem as quickly as possible.

However, if all attempts fail, a complaint is filed by the lender in the court for the county in which the property is located, and a summons is issued to the borrowers. This initiates the foreclosure process.

Simultaneous to this activity, a title search is made to determine the identities of all the parties having an interest in the collateral property, and a *lis pendens* (literally, a legal action pending) is filed with the court, giving notice to the world of the pending foreclosure action.

Notice is sent to all parties having an interest in the property, requesting that they appear in court in order to defend their interests, or else they will be foreclosed (the literal definition we mentioned earlier) from any future rights by judgment of the court. It is vitally important for the complainant lender to notify all junior lien holders of the foreclosure action so they will not be enjoined from participation in the property auction. If junior lien holders are not given proper notice, they acquire the right to file suit on their own at some future time.

Jurisdiction

Depending on the number of days required by the presiding jurisdiction for public notice to be given to inform any and all persons having an unrecorded interest in the subject property that a foreclosure suit is imminent, and depending on the availability of a court date, the complaint is eventually aired before a presiding judge. In most instances, the defendant borrower does not appear in court unless special circumstances are presented in defense of the default.

Those creditors who do appear to present their claims are recognized and noted, and a sale of the property at a public auction by a court-appointed referee or the sheriff is ordered by means of a judgment decree. The proceeds from the sale will be used to satisfy the parties named in the judgment. In Texas the borrower's right to redeem the property continues for a reasonable time after the sale.

In a judical foreclosure, a junior lien holder's interest in the property is not automatically eliminated. If the junior lien holder did not join in the foreclosure suit, the property is sold subject to the junior lien. If, however, the junior lien holder was a party to the foreclosure suit, this interest ends at the sale in the same way as the senior lien holder's interest does.

Insured Conventional Mortgage Foreclosure

Under the terms of the insurance policies of most private mortgage guarantee companies (private mortgage insurance [PMI]), a default is interpreted to be nonpayment for four months. Within 10 days of default, the lender is required to notify the private mortgage insurer, who will then decide whether to instruct the lender to foreclose.

When an insured conventional mortgage is foreclosed, the lender who is insured is the original bidder at the public auction of the collateral property. Under these circumstances, the successful bidder-lender files notice with the insurance company within 60 days after the legal proceedings have transpired.

Loss Recovery

If the insurance company is confident of recovering any losses by purchasing the collateral property from the lender and then reselling it, it will reimburse the lender for the total amount of the lender's bid and receive title to the property.

If, however, the private mortgage insurance company does not foresee any possibility for recovery, it may elect to pay the lender the agreed-upon amount of insurance, and the lender retains ownership of the property. The lender then sells the property to recover any balance still unpaid.

Remember that in any and all cases of judical foreclosure and sale, any ownership rights acquired by the successful bidder at the foreclosure auction will still be subject to the statutory redemption rights of the defaulted mortgagor. A fee simple absolute title cannot vest in the bidder until these redemption rights have expired. A property title vests, or becomes valid, when you receive full ownership rights in a property. Another way to say this is that once there is a vesting of the title, your interest in the property cannot be revoked.

FHA-Insured Mortgage Foreclosure

Foreclosures on FHA (Federal Housing Administration)–insured mortgages originate with the filing of Form 2068, Notice of Default by the lender. This form must be given to the local FHA administrative office within 60 days of default. The notice describes the reasons for the mortgagor's delinquency, such as death, illness, marital difficulties, income loss, excessive financial obligations, employment transfer, or military service.

In many cases involving delinquent FHA-insured mortgages, loan counselors from the local FHA office will attempt to design an agreement between the lender and the borrower for adjustments to the loan conditions in order to prevent foreclosure. The most common technique used in circumstances in which default is beyond the borrower's control, but deemed curable, is forbearance of foreclosure.

Default Not Cured

If the problems causing the default are solved within a one-year period, the lender informs the local FHA office of that fact. If not, a default status report is filed, and the lender must initiate foreclosure proceedings. If the bids at the foreclosure auction are less than the unpaid mortgage balance, the lender is expected to bid the debt, take title to the property, and present it to the FHA along with a claim for insurance, which may be paid in cash or in government securities. In some cases, with prior FHA approval, the lender may assign the defaulted mortgage directly to the FHA before the final foreclosure action in exchange for insurance benefits (we will talk about assigning in Chapter 15).

In any case, if the property can be sold easily at a price that would repay the loan in full, the lender simply would sell the property after bidding at the auction and would not apply for FHA compensation. If the FHA ends up as the owner of the property, the collateral may be sold "as is." The FHA may repair or refurbish (fix up) the property if it feels the property can be resold at a higher price and minimize the losses to FHA.

VA-Guaranteed Mortgage Foreclosure

Unlike the FHA-insured mortgage, whereby a lender's entire risk is recovered from the insurance benefits, a Veterans Administration (VA) loan is similar to a privately insured loan in that a lender receives only the top portion of the outstanding loan balance, up to a statutory limit. In the event of a delinquency of more than three months on a VA loan, the lender must file proper notification with the local VA office, which may then elect to bring the loan current if it wishes.

If this occurs, the VA can come against the defaulting veteran for repayment of the funds advanced. Subrogation rights are given the lender against the mortgagor for the amount advanced. This means that the VA claim against the defaulting veteran takes priority over the rights of the lender to these funds.

Like the FHA

Much like the FHA, VA lenders are required to make every effort to help the borrower through forbearance, payment adjustments, a deed in lieu of foreclosure (more about this shortly), or other acceptable solutions. Actual foreclosure is considered only as a last resort.

In the event of a foreclosure the lender usually will be the original bidder at the auction and will submit a claim for losses to the local VA office. The VA then has the option to pay the unpaid balance, interest, and court costs, if any, and take title to the property.

Or the VA can require that the lender keep the property and will pay the lender the difference between the determined value of the property on the date of the foreclosure and the mortgage balance. The latter alternative is usually chosen when the property is badly deteriorated, reinforcing the importance for a lender to supervise the condition of the collateral property.

Second Mortgage Foreclosure

Defaults of second mortgages and other junior mortgages are handled exactly in the same manner as conventional first mortgages. Here, however, the relationship is usually between two individuals rather than between an institutional lender and an individual borrower.

A second mortgagee will usually seek the counsel of an attorney to manage the foreclosure process against a second mortgagor. The delinquent borrower will be requested to cure the problem within a certain time period. If a cure cannot be accomplished, notice is given to all persons having an interest in the property, and the attorney then files for judical foreclosure.

The second mortgagee generally is the original bidder at the public sale and secures ownership of the collateral property subject to the lien of the existing first mortgage. They can then continue to maintain the integrity of this first mortgage by making any payments required, while seeking to sell the collateral to eliminate, or at least offset, any losses.

Deficiency Judgments

If the proceeds from a foreclosure sale are not sufficient to recover the outstanding loan balance plus the costs incurred as a consequence of default and interest to date, a lender may, in most states, sue on the mortgage for the deficiency.

If the foreclosure is by court order, the judge normally awards the lender a judgment against the debtor in the amount of the deficiency. If a power of sale foreclosure took place, the lender must then file suit against the debtor to collect any deficiency.

Texas

In Texas a lender would consider several things before pursuing legal action for a deficiency balance since the amount of the deficiency and the ability of the debtor to pay after the suit would be important factors.

The homestead laws in Texas, and most other states, would protect most of the debtor's basic possessions from this type of judgment. In most cases a defaulted borrower does not have any nonexempt assets to make up this deficiency. Otherwise, they would have been put to use in order to prevent the default in the first place.

Current Trend

The current trend is to rely less on collecting deficiencies and more on limiting a borrower's personal liability on a real estate loan to the equity in the collateral property. Especially on purchase money loans, lenders may be limited to recovering only the collateral property and nothing more.

One reason for this trend is the tendency of a deficiency judgment to penalize those borrowers who make good on their debts. Because such judgments can become liens against any property a borrower holds or may acquire in the future, dishonest debtors may avoid payment by simply making certain they do not own any property in their own names.

Summary

This chapter provided an overview of the foreclosure process. By far the greatest number of real estate financing arrangements do not result in problems leading to foreclosure. Rising property values coupled with the systematic repayment of loans create measurable equity positions for the borrower. A troubled borrower can, in most problem situations, arrange to dispose of assets and thus maintain financial equilibrium.

This is what gives you, as a real estate investor, an opportunity to help someone in financial distress and still make a profit. When misfortune cannot be averted and foreclosure develops as the sole remedy, this may provide the motivation to the borrower to be open to your help.

Lender Adjustments

A lender will usually attempt to adjust the conditions of a loan in order to help a troubled borrower over short-term difficulties. Delinquent mortgage payments are the most common cause for a default. The nonpayment of property taxes or hazard insurance premiums, lack of adequate maintenance, and allowing priority liens to take effect are also cause for default.

To offset the possibility of a foreclosure on delinquent mortgages, many lenders will exercise forbearance and waive the principal portion of a loan payment for a while or even extend a moratorium on the full monthly payment until a borrower can better arrange their finances. Other adjustments in terms of a delinquent mortgage that might aid the defaulted borrower include an extension of time or a recasting of the loan to reflect the borrower's current ability to pay under circumstances of financial distress.

Deed in Lieu of Foreclosure

Sometimes all efforts at adjusting the terms of a mortgage to solve a borrower's problems fail. A lender may then attempt to sell the loan. This creates further opportunities for you as a real estate investor. If the lender cannot find a buyer willing and able to buy the loan, the lender may seek to secure a voluntary transfer of title to the property from the borrower. This action prevents the possibly costly and time-consuming process of foreclosure.

By executing either a quitclaim deed or a grant deed, a borrower can eliminate the stigma of a foreclosure suit, maintain a respectable credit rating, and avoid the possibility of a deficiency judgment. Real estate lenders are fully aware of the difficulties with evictions and the costs and time involved in a full foreclosure process. Most often, the lender encourages a hopelessly defaulted borrower to transfer a deed voluntarily.

However, the lender must take care to be protected against any future claims of fraud or duress by the borrower. We will talk about this further when we discuss negotiating with the seller in pre-foreclosure in Chapter 8. In addition, the lender must be aware of the possibility of the existence of any other liens against the property. A quitclaim deed does not remove junior liens as does a completed foreclosure.

Use this chapter as your reference guide. In Chapter 3 we will show you how buying foreclosures allows you to acquire real estate at a wholesale price.

CHAPTER 3

Why Buy Foreclosures?

Foreclosures come in all shapes and sizes. Any property that has a real estate loan attached to it is a foreclosure waiting to happen. Borrowers get behind in their mortgage payments for all sorts of reasons. What is worse, people can lose their property to a foreclosure without having any real estate loans attached to the property.

If you don't pay your local property taxes, your local taxing authority can place a lien against your property. If you don't pay the property taxes within a certain period of time after the lien is filed, then the local taxing authority sells your property at a foreclosure sale for the back taxes.

You can own your property free and clear (no real estate loans) and be sued. If you lose the lawsuit, your property can be taken to satisfy the judgment. If you cannot pay the judgment, your property will be sold at a sheriff's sale to the highest bidder.

You can be current on your monthly real estate loan payments or own your property free and clear. You can be current on your local property taxes. You are not even being sued. However, you are in trouble with the Internal Revenue Service (IRS). They place a tax lien against your property. Eventually, if you don't work something out with the IRS, they will seize your property and sell it at a foreclosure sale.

All of these foreclosure events create opportunities for you as a real estate investor. From our Quick Cash strategy point of view, foreclosures provide the possibility to flip either the property or the real estate contracts associated with the property. The idea is for you to get in and get out quickly. We are going to show you how to make a profit with no money of yours tied up in the deal.

Four Reasons to Buy Foreclosures

We are going to give you four reasons to buy foreclosures. One of these reasons by itself is enough to make foreclosures a good investment. When you buy foreclosures, you are buying wholesale real estate, you are buying from a wholesale seller, you have less competition than buying retail property, and you have the opportunity to make Quick Cash.

Reason 1: Buying Wholesale Real Estate

Foreclosures are by definition wholesale real estate. Why would you want to pay retail for anything that you can buy wholesale? Real estate is the same way. When you are buying foreclosures, you are buying real estate at a wholesale price. And since real estate is the highest-priced commodity that people buy, when you buy real estate wholesale, you have an opportunity to make a lot of money.

You might think that foreclosure properties are run down or in poor shape. While this is certainly the case for some of the foreclosure properties that we have been involved with, it is not always so. You might also think foreclosure properties are in bad neighborhoods. Again, while that can be the case, we have found foreclosures in some very nice neighborhoods that were in very good condition.

Real Estate Lenders Ninety-five percent of the foreclosure market begins and ends with real estate lenders. When you understand how lenders operate, you will increase the likelihood of being successful with foreclosure investing. There are two keys: (1) Lenders get the money they make real estate loans with at a wholesale interest rate, and (2) lenders only make wholesale real estate loans (usually no more than an 80 percent loan-to-value).

Let's look at how real estate lenders operate in the real estate market. Real estate lenders make money by loaning money. How lenders get the money to loan is from people like you and us. When people put money in the bank, the bank pays those people interest or rent for their money. When the bank loans money to someone to buy real estate, it loans the money for the real estate loan at a higher interest rate than the bank pays in interest to its customers.

Wholesale Interest You could say that the bank pays a wholesale interest rate to get its money and then receives a retail interest rate when it loans its money. For example, a bank may pay 3 percent interest to its customers for certificates of deposit (CDs). Then the bank turns around and loans the money from the certificates of deposit to real estate borrowers for real estate loans at 7 percent interest.

The bank makes money on the spread between the wholesale interest rate it pays on the CDs and the retail interest rate it charges on the real estate loans.

Rule of 72 This is a good place to teach you the Rule of 72. The Rule of 72 states that whatever annual rate of return you receive on your investment, real estate or otherwise, your investment will double in the number of years you get as the answer to dividing the rate of return into 72.

The Rule of 72 assumes you leave the investment return with the investment each year so you are compounding your investment return. We will assume your investment is in a tax-free or tax-deferred vehicle.

Real estate appreciation works well with the Rule of 72. If your property appreciated 6 percent annually, it would double in value in 12 years (6 goes into 72 12 times).

But back to the real estate lender. If you receive 3 percent annual interest on $200,000 worth of CDs, then, according to the Rule of 72, your $200,000 will become $400,000 in 24 years (3 goes into 72 24 times). If the real estate lender receives 7 percent annual interest on $200,000 worth of real estate loans, then according to the Rule of 72, their $200,000 will become $400,000 in 10 years (7 goes into 72 10 times).

Certificates of Deposit	**Real Estate Loans**
$200,000 @ 3% Interest	$200,000 @ 7% Interest
72 ÷ 3 = 24 Years	72 ÷ 7 = 10 Years
Doubles to	Doubles to
$400,000	$400,000

What is truly amazing about these numbers is if we look at them over the course of a 30-year real estate loan. Your $200,000 in CDs will double once to $400,000 in 24 years. Over the next six years (from 24 years to 30 years), your $400,000 will become $500,000.

What do you think will happen to the bank's $200,000? The bank's $200,000 will double to $400,000 after 10 years, as we have already noted. The $400,000 will double to $800,000 in another 10 years (20 years total). The $800,000 will double to $1,600,000 in another 10 years (30 years total). The lender will have to give $500,000 to you for your $200,000 in CDs plus interest. The lender will make $1,100,000 profit!

Certificates of Deposit	**Real Estate Loans**
$200,000 @ 3% Interest	$200,000 @ 7% Interest
In 30 Years	In 30 Years
Becomes	Becomes
$500,000	$1,600,000

Now you know why real estate lenders want to be in the real estate-lending business. They make so much money on the interest rate spread. Real estate lenders do not want to be in the real estate-owning business.

Wholesale Loans Real estate lenders will only loan 80 percent of the appraised value of the real estate to protect themselves in the event the borrower defaults on their loan payments. In other words, a real estate lender will only make a wholesale real estate loan. The amount the lender loans is called the loan-to-value ratio. How much money would a bank loan on a property that was appraised (valued) for $200,000?

Loan-to-Value Ratio

Appraised Value	$200,000
Maximum Loan Percentage	× 80%
Maximum Loan Amount	$160,000

As you can see from these numbers, real estate lenders protect themselves by making sure they have a 20 percent cushion between the appraised value, $200,000, and the loan value, $160,000. This $40,000 cushion is typically the borrower's down payment on the property. Even if the borrower defaults to the tune of $10,000, the lender is protected.

Lender Protection

Appraised Value	$200,000
Maximum Loan Amount	− $160,000
Default Amount	− $ 10,000
Lender Protection	$ 30,000
Lender Loss	0

What about real estate lenders who loan 90 percent or 95 percent of the retail value? Won't that put them in jeopardy in the event of a default?

That's where private mortgage insurance (PMI) companies step in. For an insurance premium paid by the borrower, the private mortgage insurer will insure the real estate lender for any defaults above an 80 percent loan-to-value ratio.

Let's say the borrower received a 90 percent loan from the lender ($180,000) and made only a 10 percent down payment ($20,000) on the same $200,000 property.

Loan-to-Value Ratio

Appraised Value	$200,000
Loan Percentage	× 90%
Loan Amount	$180,000

With the same $10,000 borrower default, the lender still has $10,000 of protection.

Lender Protection

Appraised Value	$200,000
Maximum Loan Amount	− $180,000
Default Amount	− $ 10,000
Lender Protection	$ 10,000
Lender Loss	0

Even if the borrower defaulted in the amount of $25,000, the PMI would pick up the additional $5,000 beyond the borrower's $20,000 equity (down payment).

Private Mortgage Insurance

Appraised Value	$200,000
Maximum Loan Amount	− $180,000
Default Amount	− $ 25,000
Lender Protection	($ 5,000)
Private Mortgage Insurance	$ 5,000
Lender Loss	0

Reason 2: Buying from a Wholesale Seller

It is important to identify who sells wholesale property. Once you know who the sellers are, you can prepare your strategy to achieve the best results. There are only three sellers of foreclosure property.

Two of the sellers have a big financial stake in the property. One of the sellers has no financial stake in the property. Two of the sellers are professional sellers. One of the sellers is not.

Buying from the Seller in Distress Sellers in distress have a big financial stake in the property. Not only will it destroy their credit if their property goes to a foreclosure sale, but they will lose all their equity in the property. And, obviously, the seller in distress is not a professional seller.

We'll use some of the numbers we have already shown to illustrate our point. The appraised value of the property is $200,000. The loan amount on the property is $160,000. The borrower is in default in the amount of $10,000. The borrower's equity position before the default is $40,000.

Where does the borrower's $10,000 default amount come out of? As we have already seen, the $10,000 default amount comes out of the borrower's $40,000 equity. The further the borrower gets behind in their mortgage payments, the more of the borrower's remaining equity is eaten up.

Your mission with sellers in distress is to show them how to avoid the foreclosure sale. We will spend a chapter teaching you how to do this (see Chapter 7). You are going to become an educator to the seller in distress. You will make an appointment with them. At the appointment you will educate them on their eight foreclosure options.

For their sake, we hope that you will be able to get the information to them before it is too late. One of the foreclosure options you will present is for them to sell you their equity. You can only pay them a wholesale price. They will get some of their equity back if they work with you. If the property goes to the foreclosure sale, they will get none of their equity back.

You might offer them $9,000 for their remaining $30,000 equity. Remember, you will still have to come up with an additional $10,000 to make up the default to the lender. You would now have $19,000 in the property ($9,000 to the seller and $10,000 to the lender).

You would also get the property subject to the $160,000 loan. Your total in the property would be $179,000. The property is worth $200,000. You have a $21,000 profit potential, which is more than a 100 percent return on your $19,000 investment.

Profit Potential

Loan Amount	$160,000
Buy Seller's Equity	$ 9,000
Default Amount	$ 10,000
Amount in Property	$179,000
Appraised Value	$200,000
Profit Potential	$ 21,000
$21,000 ÷ $19,000	= 111%

Buying at the Foreclosure Sale Foreclosure sales are conducted at a public auction. The highest bidder gets the property. The seller at the foreclosure sale is a trustee or representative of the lender. So the seller at the foreclosure sale is really like an auctioneer. They are professional sellers. Yet they do not have any financial stake in the property. They are just doing their job.

Once it gets to the foreclosure sale, the owners are out of luck. If you have not been able to help them, or work out a purchase for their equity, the owners will lose all of their equity at the foreclosure sale.

You must have cash or cashier's checks to bid at the foreclosure sale. It is best to check with the foreclosure-sale seller before the actual foreclosure-sale date to find out how the seller wants payment.

Credit Bid The opening bid is called a credit bid. The credit bid is put forward by the trustee or the representative of the lender. The credit bid is the total of the remaining loan balance, payments in default, and any costs associated with the foreclosure sale. If no one bids above the credit bid, then the lender winds up owning the property. Any bid made above the credit bid has to be made in cash. Let's say the foreclosure sale expenses are $1,900. What would the opening credit bid be? Again, we will continue to use the same numbers we have used throughout this chapter.

Opening Credit Bid

Loan Amount	$160,000
Default Amount	$ 10,000
Foreclosure Expenses	$ 1,900
Credit Bid	$171,900

Winning the Bid What if you bid one dollar more than the opening credit bid? If you could buy the property at the foreclosure sale for

$171,901, would that be a better deal than if you could have bought the property from the owner before the foreclosure sale for $179,000?

The answer is that it depends. While it certainly looks like getting the property at the foreclosure sale for $7,099 less is the better deal, maybe it isn't the better deal. This is a price-versus-terms conversation.

You get a better price at the foreclosure sale. But you have to come up with almost $172,000! Buying from the seller, you didn't get as good a price—$179,000. But you only have $19,000 in the deal. Will that $7,000 lower price be worth tying up an additional $153,000?

Buying from the Lender What about buying from the lender after the foreclosure sale? Usually, the lender has the biggest financial stake in the property. After all, they originally made an 80 percent loan to the borrower to buy the property. Can you get a better deal from the lender once the property goes out of the lender's loan portfolio and into the lender's property portfolio?

Lenders' property portfolios are called real estate–owned portfolios, or REOs. Real estate lenders are in the business of making real estate loans. Real estate lenders are not in the business of owning real estate.

Although lenders want to sell their REOs for as much as possible, they want to move these REO properties as quickly as possible. After all, we know what they are going to do with the money they get from selling the property. They are going to make another real estate loan!

Depending on the real estate lender, you may be able to pick up this REO property from them in the neighborhood of $155,000 to $165,000. Sounds like the best deal in the price department. What about the terms department? Ah, there is the rub. Are you going to have to put up a lot of cash and qualify for a new loan?

While real estate lenders are professional sellers, sometimes their own bureaucracy gets in the way of them making an effective deal. Our recommendation to you is to work with several lenders' REO departments and see what happens. Our overall recommendation is to work out a deal with the seller in distress. Then you have more Quick Cash options available.

Reason 3: Less Competition Than Retail

As competitive as the foreclosure market may seem, it is less competitive than the retail market. There are fewer people involved in the foreclosure market. Of the total number of real estate mortgages, a maximum of 2 percent of them will be in the foreclosure process at any one time. Once you become familiar with the material in this book, you will know more than 98 percent of the people trying to make money investing in foreclosures.

Hell, you will know more about foreclosures than 99 percent of the attorneys out there. (Maybe we should retract that endorsement about you knowing more than 99 percent of the attorneys.) The point is that we think one of the best reasons to check out the foreclosure scene is that there is very little knowledgeable competition.

Reason 4: Make Quick Cash

You can make Quick Cash in the foreclosure arena. We recommend you work with the seller in distress before the foreclosure process gets too far down the line. We call this the pre-foreclosure stage. Once you make a deal with the seller in distress, then you flip your foreclosure real estate contract.

Assign Foreclosure Contracts You may find it easier to assign foreclosure contracts than it is to assign non-foreclosure contracts. When people in general, and real estate investors in particular, hear the word *foreclosure,* they automatically think there might be a good deal here. When you drop the word *foreclosure* at a social gathering, everyone turns around to catch the conversation.

Rent Busters In the 1990s in California there was a company called Rent Busters. It offered foreclosed homes to buyers for no down payments. The concept was simple. The company would advertise for people to find foreclosure deals.

The company was paid $1,500 by a client to take the client to a foreclosure sale to buy the client a property. The client had to agree to go to 10 fore-closure sales. If, after going to 10 foreclosure sales, Rent Busters had not bought the client a property, the client got the $1,500 back.

If Rent Busters did buy a property at one of the 10 foreclosure sales, the client's $1,500 would be applied to closing costs. The company would go to the foreclosure sale and buy the property. It would pay no more than 80 percent of the retail value. Of course, since the company was buying the property at the foreclosure sale, it would pay cash.

Then Rent Busters would sell the property to the people who had brought the foreclosure to them. They would sell the property to the client for no money down. Rent Busters would carry the down payment back in a promissory note secured by a second mortgage.

The client would get a new 80 percent loan on the property. The proceeds of the loan would go to Rent Busters as the seller. This would replenish the cash that Rent Busters used to purchase the property at the foreclosure sale. Then the down payment financing would become the profit for Rent Busters collectable over the agreed time frame.

Example Let's say Rent Busters got a $200,000 property for $160,000 at the foreclosure sale and financed the $40,000 down payment for the buyer for three years at 10 percent annual interest.

Foreclosure Sale

Retail Value	$200,000
Foreclosure Price	$160,000
Equity for Rent Busters	$ 40,000

Sale to Client

Purchase Price	$200,000
New Financing	$160,000
Seller Financing	$ 40,000

Profit to Rent Busters

Seller Financing	$40,000
10% for 3 Years	$12,000
Gross Profit	$52,000

Summary

When you buy foreclosures, you are buying wholesale real estate, you are buying from a wholesale seller, you have less competition than buying retail property, and you have the opportunity to make Quick Cash.

In the next chapter we will teach you how to buy foreclosures. The key is getting to the seller in distress before another investor does. Your goal is to help them out of their foreclosure situation and find a great real estate investment for yourself that you can flip for Quick Cash.

CHAPTER 4

How to Buy Foreclosures

In this chapter we will teach you how to buy foreclosures. Most of you think that buying a foreclosure has to occur at a foreclosure sale. Foreclosure sales are usually conducted on the courthouse steps in the county the property is located. We will teach you how to buy a foreclosure on the courthouse steps. We will also teach you how to buy a foreclosure before it gets to the courthouse steps.

At one of the recent courthouse foreclosure sales we attended, there were over one thousand properties being auctioned in one day! This was the number of foreclosure sales for our county for one month! It was a total zoo. There were at least five hundred people trying to figure out what to do, whom to talk to, and where to bid. We bought nothing that day.

We are going to start you out with a better idea. Let's talk to the property owner who is in financial distress. They are headed down the road to a full-blown foreclosure. If we can identify these owners in distress early enough, we may be able to help them at the same time we help ourselves.

Owners in Financial Distress

There are two time periods to work with owners in financial distress. There is the time period before the lender files a notice of default at the county recorder's office. And there is the time period after the lender files a notice of default at the county recorder's office but before the foreclosure sale takes place.

If you are able to develop a rapport with the owners and make a foreclosure options presentation to them, you will have a good chance of helping the owner in distress as well as making a good deal for yourself. We present the following guidelines to help you when dealing with the owner.

Guidelines

1. Know the Area Make sure you are familiar with the properties that have sold. In other words, know the comps. Get sales information from title insurance companies. Talk with neighbors of the owner and to local real estate agents. Make sure you know value in your target area. (See Chapter 8 for a complete discussion on value.)

2. Inspect the Property Ask the owner to show you around the property. Take notice of faulty conditions or red flags, which may indicate problems with the property. Use a clipboard and write down your observations. This will serve as a memory aid for you. It will also show the owner that you are serious about the property.

3. Arrive with a List of Questions Dress appropriately for the meeting. Don't overdress or arrive in too fancy a vehicle. Have a calm demeanor. Don't seem overly anxious to make a deal. Treat the owner with respect, diplomacy, and understanding. Listen more than you talk.

Take the time to develop a rapport before you get into your questions. Be prepared to discuss details with the owner that will make it clear what the owner needs financially. In other words, discover the owner's true motivation and needs. Ask the questions in a friendly manner.

4. Avoid Making Any Proposals There are no oral agreements in real estate. At this initial meeting you are gathering information about the owner and the property. Any proposal you make should be in writing and done when all the decision makers are present. This may occur immediately after you have inspected the property or at a later scheduled foreclosure presentation.

5. Use Your Foreclosure Options Presentation For best results, follow a written outline when discussing the owner's options. We recommend setting up an evening appointment for your foreclosure options presentation.

Your goals are to have the owner understand the foreclosure process, clearly see the owner's options, recognize your knowledge of the subject, and put together a mutually beneficial contract.

Setting an Appointment with the Owner

When setting the appointment with the owner for the foreclosure presentation, plan on only one presentation per evening. This is important because some owners will take longer to make a decision than others. In circumstances where you have planned appointments too close together, each one will be rushed, and opportunities to acquire properties may be missed.

No appointment should be set unless all owners will be present. If you get to the appointment and one of the owners cannot be present, reschedule for another time. Otherwise, you are wasting your time.

It is important that the owner feels relaxed and is able to discuss their situation with you at the stated time. Accordingly, as with any real estate contract presentation, the time for the appointment should be at an hour when distractions such as kids and favorite TV shows are not competition.

Let's turn our attention to your initial phone conversation with the owner. The purpose of the conversation is to set an appointment with the owner. At this appointment you will make the foreclosure options presentation.

Phone Appointment Script *Hello, my name is __________, and I am calling because I may have an interest in buying your property. Are you the owner? What is your name?*

Wait for their response. If they are not the owner, ask to speak to the owner.

According to public records, I understand that your loan may be in trouble, and that you might be able to use some help. Is this a convenient time to talk?

Wait for their response. If they say no, ask when would be a good time for you to call back.

As I said, my name is ________, and I am a private real estate investor who makes it my practice to understand the foreclosure process and how to avoid it. My interest in your property stems from the fact that I can often find a good investment by talking to people who have a problem loan.

I sometimes find that they have a desire to sell their property at a price that will save some of their equity, help them protect their credit, and, at the same time, I may find a property to acquire.

I have developed a presentation that will show you your many options to avoid foreclosure. I recognize that nearly 9 out of 10 owners will be able to save their property with this information.

I am willing to share this information with you without cost or obligation. The properties I do buy have made it worth my time to help many property owners such as yourself avoid foreclosure entirely. Do you have an interest in finding out about the eight options you have with regard to your pending foreclosure?

At this point you have aroused the curiosity of the owner and setting the time for an appointment should almost be automatic.

I have time on my schedule tonight or tomorrow night. Since time is of the essence for some of these foreclosure options, would tonight or tomorrow night be better for you?

Wait for their response.

Would seven o'clock or eight o'clock be better for you?

Wait for their response.

After you have set a time ask this last question: *Do you have younger children at home?*

Wait for their response. If the say they have younger children, say:

I recognize that it is important that parents spend quality time with their children, and I do not wish to disturb that. Is there a time, perhaps after your children have gone to bed, that we can talk?

Such consideration will make an impression on the owner, show great respect for their family, and assure you of an uninterrupted appointment.

At the Appointment

Your purpose at the appointment is to create a mutually beneficial solution to the foreclosure problem for you and the property owner. After you have no more than five minutes of chitchat conversation during which you are building rapport with the owner, you should begin your foreclosure presentation at the owner's kitchen table.

We recommend you sit with your back to an outside wall. That way the owner(s) are giving you their full attention and will not be distracted by what is going on in the rest of the house. Please ask that TV or loud music that can be heard in the kitchen be turned off or down.

Ask questions first. Expand on your knowledge of the owners' situation. Make sure you understand the owners' situation completely before you propose any solutions to their foreclosure problem. Then make your foreclosure options presentation. We give you the complete foreclosure options presentation in Chapter 7. For now we will just sketch the foreclosure options for you.

Foreclosure Options The eight foreclosure options are reinstatement, redemption, deed in lieu of foreclosure, legal delay, bankruptcy, renegotiate, sell the property, or do nothing. Some of these foreclosure options are time-sensitive. Others require an expenditure of money that the owner probably doesn't have.

By analyzing the owners' situation, you can determine the best solution. If they have the ability to get their hands on some money, they may be able to reinstate, redeem, or renegotiate their loan with the lender. If they want to go the legal route, they may seek a legal delay or file bankruptcy.

If they have enough time, the owners may be able to sell the property or negotiate a deed in lieu of foreclosure with the lender. If the owners do nothing, they will lose their property at the foreclosure sale.

Foreclosure Solutions You are the solution to the owners' foreclosure problem. Let's assume the owners have neither the money nor the time to make something positive happen on their own with the information you have shared with them. This is where you step in and propose some very creative solutions.

The simplest solution is for you to "buy" the owner's equity. The owner would give you a quitclaim deed to the property. You would reinstate the loan and own the property. Or you could flip the property for Quick Cash and let the new buyer work things out with the lender.

Buy the Equity Let's say the property is worth $210,000. The loan balance is $150,000. The owner is behind $12,000 in payments. The owner's equity position is $48,000.

Owner's Equity

Property Value	\$210,000
Loan Balance	\$150,000
Behind in Payments	\$ 12,000
Owner's Remaining Equity	\$ 48,000

You offer the owner \$11,000 for the remaining equity. You, or the new buyer, will have to come up with an additional \$12,000 to reinstate the loan. You would be paying \$173,000 for the property. If the property has a value of \$210,000, this looks like you have \$37,000 in equity.

Purchase Price

Loan Balance	\$150,000
Behind in Payments	\$ 12,000
Equity Offer	\$ 11,000
Purchase Price	\$173,000

Equity Sharing Let's get more creative. We have the same owners with the same numbers. They really want to keep their property. They have had a temporary financial setback. They feel that if they can buy some time and get some financial help they will be able to keep their property.

You propose paying the \$12,000 they are behind in their payments to the lender in return for a 75 percent equity position in the property. Remember, the equity in the property will be \$60,000 after the loan is reinstated (\$210,000 property value minus the \$150,000 loan balance).

You will pay 25 percent of the future monthly loan payments, and the owners will pay 75 percent of the future monthly loan payments. You will pay \$12,000 cash and have a \$45,000 equity position in the property. The property owners will retain a \$15,000 equity position in the property.

This deal is a win for you and a win for the property owners. Plus, instead of having just a renter living in the property who may tear the property up, you have co-owners who have a stake in the property.

Equity Sharing

Your Equity	*Owner's Equity*
Property Equity: \$60,000	Property Equity: \$60,000
Equity Percentage: × 75%	Equity Percentage: × 25%
Equity Position: \$45,000	Equity Position: \$15,000

Equity Sharing Redux Equity sharing is a way in which two or more parties, one being an owner-occupant and the other being a real estate investor, pool their funds to buy or hold a property. There are many ways that equity sharing can work. In the usual equity-sharing agreement, a non–owner-occupant puts up the down payment, and the owner-occupant, in effect, becomes the tenant.

The owner-occupant will pay the fair-market rent and both the owner-occupant and non–owner-occupant split all the expenses of the property based on their ownership percentage. It does not have to be 50-50 (see previous example).

From a tax point of view, the owner-occupant will usually get the write-off of their share of the interest on the loan and the property taxes. The non–owner-occupant will include half of the rent as income and deduct their share of the interest, property taxes, and all expenses on the property and depreciation on their ownership interest.

The portion of the Internal Revenue Code (IRC) that relates to equity sharing is section 280A. One of its main purposes is to make sure that fair-market rent was charged in an equity-share arrangement, especially between family members. Section 280A is somewhat vague and provides no definitive guidelines on equity sharing.

Additionally, thus far, there have been no court cases, few rulings, and no specific regulations dealing with the subject. Your tax advisor should be included in any decision you make regarding equity sharing. We include a synopsis of section 280A for your review because of its specific foreclosure application.

IRC 280A Equity sharing can be used in foreclosure by having the non–owner-occupant supply the cash needed to reinstate the loan and share in the monthly operating expenses. Owning half of the property, and therefore being obligated for only half of the expenses of the property, will be a great relief to the owner-occupant, allowing them to maintain an equity interest in the property and keep a foreclosure off their credit record.

The non–owner-occupant owns a portion of a property with a tenant owner, which should eliminate the need for a property manager. A buy-out or refinance arrangement can be structured in the "Shared Equity Financing Agreement" to the satisfaction of all parties concerned.

Reverse Lease Option (Sale Leaseback with Option to Purchase) As a final creative solution we give you the reverse lease option. When we think of lease options, we think of leasing the property with an option to purchase the property at some point in the future at some agreed-upon price.

A foreclosure twist on this technique is to purchase the property in default and lease it back to the owner. You also give them an option to purchase the property at some point in the future at some agreed-upon price. If the loan has a due-on-sale clause, you should discuss it with the lender. Keep in mind that most lenders do not want more property in their REO portfolio and will probably not call the loan.

The agreed-upon future price should include any cash you put into the property to reinstate the loan plus any negative cash flow (if applicable) and an acceptable return on your investment. As with the equity-sharing arrangement, consult with your attorney for assistance in structuring the transaction.

At the Sale

Georgetown, Texas

We conclude this chapter with one of our experiences at a real estate auction in Georgetown, Texas. While this was not a foreclosure sale, we present it here as an example of how to bid and when to bid.

We were in Georgetown doing a marketing promotion and were doing some sightseeing. We drove past an old Victorian home with signs in the front yard announcing an estate sale for the weekend. We stopped to look and discovered two things.

An estate auctioneer had rented the vacant property and brought their inventory of estate-sale items to this property. The auctioneer wanted the ambiance of the property to create an atmosphere for the estate sale. We actually thought this was a very smart marketing ploy.

We also discovered that on Sunday afternoon at the conclusion of the estate sale auction, the auctioneer was going to hold an auction for the property. This was now becoming very exciting!

We toured the house and grounds and decided to participate in the property auction. We had determined that the property needed about $150,000 in renovations. Once the work was completed, we felt the property would sell in the $450,000 to $600,000 range.

The Auction The auction was conducted in the back yard under a canopy. We registered for the auction and got our bidding number. There were 30 to 40 people sitting in chairs at the back of the auction area. We walked in and sat down toward the front so we would have an unobstructed view of the auctioneer.

The auctioneer made an announcement that there would be a bidder making bids over the phone to one of the members of the auctioneer's staff. The auctioneer then began the auction by asking for an opening bid of $400,000. When no one would bite, the auctioneer asked the bidders to make an opening bid.

The first bid was for $50,000. The second bid was for $100,000. The third bid was for $150,000. We were watching and listening and waiting. Finally there were only two bidders bidding; the bidder on the phone and one of the bidders on site. They were bidding back and forth in $5,000 increments.

The bidder on the phone bid $195,000. The auctioneer asked for a $200,000 bid. The bidder on site said nothing. The auctioneer announced "$195,000 going once. $195,000 going twice." That is when Bill raised his bid card from his lap and held it in front of him.

The auctioneer pointed at Bill and said, "$200,000." Our bid was relayed to the phone bidder. You could tell the phone bidder was stunned by our bid from the reaction of the auctioneer's staff person. Finally, they came back with a bid of $205,000. We immediately bid $210,000.

This was going to be our final bid no matter what. We had determined that we would bid no more than $210,000 before the auction started. The auctioneer asked for a $215,000 bid. None was forthcoming. The auctioneer announced "$210,000 going once. $210,000 going twice. $210,000 going three times. Sold, for $210,000."

We had won the bid. We were very happy. People came up and congratulated us. What we want you to learn is our technique for bidding. We made sure we were well situated to be seen by the auctioneer. We didn't bid until the end of the bidding process. We knew what our top bid was going to be. We didn't go over our predetermined top bid.

In the next chapter we will show you the four time periods or phases in the foreclosure process to buy foreclosures. Phase 1 is a pre-foreclosure time period before the notice of default is posted. Phase 2 is still a pre-foreclosure time period after the notice of default is posted and before the foreclosure sale occurs. Phase 3 is at the foreclosure sale. Phase 4 is after the foreclosure sale.

Our recommendation is that you buy foreclosures before the foreclosure sale. It may not be as exciting as buying at the foreclosure auction. But you will have far less competition! And you will have an opportunity to make Quick Cash.

CHAPTER 5

When to Buy Foreclosures

In this chapter we are going to show you the different times you can get involved in the real estate foreclosure market. There are four time periods or phases when you can buy foreclosures. As we have said before, when we say "buy" foreclosures, we are using the term *buy* loosely. With our Quick Cash strategy, we prefer flipping property rather than buying property.

In our book *The New Path to Real Estate Wealth: Earning Without Owning,* we emphasize flipping the paperwork of real estate. We are not interested in buying or owning anything. Because the foreclosure market is so technical, we have presented the material as if you were buying foreclosures. We will show you how to flip foreclosures no matter what time period or phase you choose to get involved in the foreclosure market.

Timing the Foreclosure Buy

In situations where the property owners are in financial distress and their property is headed to a foreclosure sale, you have four distinct time periods in which you have an opportunity to acquire the property. Each of these time periods has benefits and drawbacks.

These four time periods are (1) before the notice of default is filed or posted at the county courthouse, (2) after the notice of default is filed or posted at the county courthouse, (3) during the foreclosure sale, and (4) after the foreclosure sale when the property belongs to a new owner who is either the foreclosing lender or another real estate investor.

Let's take a look at the foreclosure timeline in Texas. While your state may have a different foreclosure timeline, you will find the same buying opportunities available. Let's see where the four time periods or phases occur on the Texas foreclosure timeline. This will help you see where the four time periods occur on your state's foreclosure timeline.

Texas Foreclosure Timeline

2 – 3 Months	20 Days		Can Be 1 Day	21 Days Minimum
No Payments	1st Official Letter	2nd Official Letter	Posting at Courthouse	Sale 1st Tuesday

Phase 1: Before the Posting of the Notice of Default

Whether the posting is called a notice of default in the case of a deed of trust or a *lis pendens* in the case of a mortgage, this marks the official beginning of the foreclosure. Once the foreclosure process begins, it may lead to the forced sale of the owners' property, the loss of their equity, and the resulting damage to their credit.

If you can make a deal with the owner before the commencement of legal action, you will help the owner reduce the negative effects of foreclosure. And you may find that you can obtain a better buy because there will be less competition from other real estate investors for the property prior to the public notice of default or the *lis pendens* being recorded at the county recorder's office.

The drawback with trying to make a deal in this time period is that you may find that the owners are not as motivated as they will be in the next time periods. We have found that owners at this point are still clinging to the unrealistic hope that a financial miracle is going to happen.

Using the Texas foreclosure timeline, this is the time period up to the posting of the notice of default at the county courthouse. The owners are several months behind in their payments. Their lender may have already sent them a warning letter. The owners are starting to feel some pressure. Your job is to show them that the pressure is only going to get more intense. If they act now with you, the pressure will dissipate.

Early Resolution Few borrowers intend to default on their loans. Sometimes economic developments beyond their control can create the situations leading to foreclosure. They may have been fired from their job. Their job may have disappeared. Interest rates may have increased on their adjustable rate mortgage and made their mortgage payments prohibitive.

Divorce, premature death, disability, illness, addiction, and accidents can all lead to foreclosure. Poor money management, like too much money in the stock market, can be a recipe for financial disaster. The result of the foreclosure can be embarrassing to the borrower, besides suffering the devastating financial consequences of losing their property and equity.

Early resolution of the pending foreclosure benefits the borrower and can produce better results for you as the real estate investor. Additionally, completing a transaction before the foreclosure period begins (once the posting occurs) can often avoid specific legislative guidelines that become restrictive on certain transactions.

Phase 2: After the Posting of the Notice of Default

Once the notice of default has been posted, there are a number of things for you to consider. First, there may be certain restrictions and legal requirements that your individual state may enforce when a property is officially in foreclosure. Second, once the notice of default is recorded, there is public knowledge of the default, and you will find you have competition from other real estate investors for the property.

Using the Texas foreclosure timeline, this is the time period after the posting of the notice of default and before the actual foreclosure sale. This can be a period of time as short as 21 days in Texas. Check with a title insurance company in your area to find out what the time period is in your state.

Legislative Requirements In California, once the notice of default is posted at the courthouse, you, as the real estate investor, have to comply with several state laws. These laws were enacted by the California legislature to protect homeowners from real estate investor sharks.

Unfortunately, as with many well-intentioned laws, this law has had unintentional negative effects. It has inhibited defaulting homeowners from being able to sell their homes to legitimate real estate investors who are trying to create a win-win situation for the defaulting homeowners and themselves. Yes, it may protect some defaulting homeowners from unscrupulous people. But it puts onerous restrictions on homeowners' property rights.

California Foreclosure Timeline

2 – 3 Months	3 – 4 Weeks		3 Months	20 Days	Next Day
No Payments	1st Official Letter	2nd Official Letter	Posting at Courthouse	Redeem Only	Sale

In California, if you are buying a property that is owner-occupied, and one- to four-dwelling units (a single-family up to a fourplex), and a notice of default has been posted against the property, you must include in your real estate purchase contract two notices required by California law.

You must include a five-day cancellation-of-contract notice and a notice informing the homeowners that they cannot be asked to sign a deed transferring title to their property to you until the five-day cancellation of-contract period expires. If you don't do this, the homeowners can come back against you and have the courts void your deal and impose fines and penalties against you.

NOTICE REQUIRED BY CALIFORNIA LAW

Until your right to cancel this contract has ended _______(buyer) or anyone working for ____________(buyer) CANNOT ask you to sign or have you sign any deed or any other document. You may

cancel this contract for the sale of your house without any penalty or obligation at any time before ___(AM/PM) on ______, 20__. See the attached notice of cancellation form for an explanation of this right.

NOTICE OF CANCELLATION

____

(Enter date contract signed)

You may cancel this contract for the sale of your house, without penalty or obligation, at any time before _______________. To cancel this transaction, personally deliver a signed and dated copy of this cancellation notice, or send a telegram to_________________ (buyer) at __________________(address)

NOT LATER THAN ___________________________________

I hereby cancel this transaction _______________________(date)

____

____

(Sellers' signatures)

Benefits and Drawbacks of the Notice of Default One benefit of the notice of default is the sense of urgency it creates for the property owner. Once the foreclosure process has begun, it is only a matter of time before the property will be sold to the highest bidder. Coupled with the ever-shrinking equity that remains for the owner as time goes by, you can often make a good investment if you can get in touch with the owner during this time period.

Of course, every other real estate investor who follows the notice-of-default postings is now aware of these properties. This can be a huge drawback to you because you now are competing with many other investors for the same properties.

However, you can turn this potential drawback into an advantage once you get in front of the owner and make your foreclosure options presentation. No one else will be interested in helping the owner like you are.

Phase 3: At the Sale

For those of you who wait until the day of the foreclosure sale to get involved, preparation is of the utmost importance. The time you spend in researching both the property and the title will pay huge dividends when you are bidding. Again, we reiterate that you must know value before you make any bids.

We suggest you attend several foreclosure sales as dry runs to get a sense of how things occur, especially with regard to the trustees conducting the sales. Perhaps even more important is going to foreclosure sales to observe your competition before you actually start bidding.

While at the foreclosure sales in which you wish to participate, observe the habits of the successful bidders. Some of these faces you will see again and again. Note their habits and what they do when they enter the bidding.

On properties bidders want, do they enter the bidding at the beginning, middle, or end? Are some of the bidders working together to squeeze out the competition? Also take note of what a bidder does when he or she folds.

The advantage of buying at the foreclosure sale is the finality of it. You will receive your money back if the owners can exercise their right of redemption. All junior liens will be wiped out. You have the protection of your state's foreclosure laws for the winning bidder. It is a can't-lose proposition for you. And you have an upside potential because you bought the property wholesale.

The big disadvantage of buying at the foreclosure sale is the fact that you have to pay cash, and a lot of it. The other disadvantage is the sheer number of other investors you may encounter who want to bid on or buy the properties you are interested in.

Phase 4: After the Foreclosure Sale

When a property does not sell at the foreclosure sale, the lender will take it back. If the lender is an institutional lender, the property will become an REO (real estate owned). Lenders are anxious to liquidate these properties. Because they are not in the resale business, lenders sometimes mishandle these properties.

To find out about a lender's REOs, don't rely on the branch manager of a bank for much help. REOs are kept quiet, and it will take some probing to discover the pearls.

Your best source for REOs may be a real estate agent who handles them in your area. An agent may specialize in REO properties and have useful contacts already in place with several lenders. Do some calling around to find out who these real estate agents are.

If you have no other contact, establish a rapport with the branch manager of your bank or savings association. Ask the manager to make an introductory call to the REO manager.

This manner of making the appointment will give you a personal introduction to the person in charge of the bank's REOs. You will not have to waste your time going up the food chain over the phone.

Private REOs What if the lender who winds up with the property after the foreclosure sale is a private lender? A private lender may have even less motivation to own the property than the institutional lenders. Typically, these lenders were owners of the property in the past. They sold the property and helped the buyer with seller carry-back financing in order to make the deal work.

They may have moved out of the area. The private lender may not want to take the time to remarket the property. What about the expenses of holding the property while the lender resells it? And the private lender certainly doesn't want to have to find a tenant and become a landlord.

We recommend you talk to the lender or the lender's representative immediately after the foreclosure sale. They may have gotten title to the property back, no money in their pockets, and be facing the prospect of having to make payments on an existing senior lien.

This can make private lenders extremely motivated to discuss a deal. Some of you may find your foreclosure-investing niche working exclusively with REO private lenders. Remember, they have made a credit bid for the amount of their loan balance, plus the back payments, plus foreclosure expenses, plus payments on the senior lien.

If no one bids, they get the title to the property. They may sell their position to you for a lot less than their credit bid once they wind up with the property. Let's look at some numbers.

Let's say the lender is in a second position with a $25,000 loan balance, $1,250 in back payments, $750 in foreclosure expenses, and five months of payments on the senior lien of $4,000.

Credit Bid

Loan Balance	$25,000
Back Payments	$ 1,250
Foreclosure Expenses	$ 750
Senior Lien Payments	$ 4,000
Credit Bid	$31,000

No one has bid above the $31,000 credit bid. You may be able to offer $15,000 cash and have the lender give you title to the property. Do you think that may be a good deal? Our answer is that it depends.

What is the value of the property? What is the amount of the senior lien? Are there other liens against the title that you will be stuck with once you have the title to the property?

Our point is that just because you are getting what looks like a good deal from the private REO lender, as with all foreclosure deals, *caveat emptor*, let the buyer beware! You still have to do your due diligence and know about the property and the condition of the title before you make an investment.

Another Real Estate Investor You may find you are able to make a deal with the real estate investor who makes the successful winning bid at the foreclosure sale. This investor may be buying the property with a plan to fix it up and put it back on the market. You didn't bid higher during the auction because you had reached your predetermined top bid. But you already have a buyer who will pay $10,000 more than the winning bid.

You could offer the other real estate investor $5,000 more than they paid to sell you the property on the spot. While they have a profitable plan, they may sell you the property for the immediate $5,000 profit. You would then flip the property to your buyer and make your own $5,000 profit.

Summary

There are four time periods or phases to invest in foreclosures. While the foreclosure timeline varies from state to state, every state's foreclosure process includes these time periods.

These four time periods are before the notice of default is filed or posted at the county courthouse, after the notice of default is filed or posted at the county courthouse, during the foreclosure sale, and after the foreclosure sale when the property belongs to a new owner who is either the foreclosing lender or another real estate investor.

You can make Quick Cash in foreclosures no matter what phase you make your investment. The key is to find your niche. Your niche is where you feel the most comfortable and confident. Your niche is also where you consistently make money. As you are getting started, try to make something happen in each foreclosure phase and discover for yourself where you belong.

In the next chapter we will teach you where to find foreclosures. There are foreclosure opportunities everywhere. There are foreclosure opportunities in a good economy and a bad economy. We will also show you how to access the largest holder of REOs in the world.

CHAPTER 6

How to Find Foreclosures

In this chapter we will teach you how to find foreclosures. You have to be a pretty good detective if you are going to be a successful real estate investor. You have to be a great detective if you are going to be successful investing in foreclosures. You are looking for the owner in distress.

We are going to give you the 13 key words or phrases that we look for when we go through classified ads, work with our personal contacts, do our own scouting, visit open houses, or work with a real estate agent. When you see or hear one or more of these words or phrases, you'll know that you have found the right seller.

Finding Properties in Pre-Foreclosure

Finding properties before the notice of default occurs can be difficult. There is no official public record available to you that would alert you to a property owner's financial troubles. Instead you have to search for clues to their financial troubles as well as being proactive seeking opportunities in the pre-foreclosure phase.

Clues to an owner in distress include deferred maintenance on a property or the look of a property being abandoned. Other clues are general lack of care by the owner or tenant or frequent official deliveries of notices to pay.

It takes a keen eye to observe some of these subtle hints to a preforeclosure condition. Networking with neighbors and service providers such as delivery companies, utility providers, and postal carriers can provide you with extra eyes.

13 Key Words or Phrases

1. Must Sell Any time you encounter the phrase *must sell,* you have come upon the right seller. It is perfectly acceptable to ask must-sell sellers why they must sell. You may discover that they are selling because they are behind on their mortgage payments.

We have heard some pretty strange reasons for selling, as well as the fairly standard legitimate reasons for selling. The point is that a seller's must-sell reason is his or her own.

2. Under Market The phrase *under market* can let you know that you have come upon the right seller and the right property. As a real estate investor you are a wholesale buyer. A property that is advertised as being under market puts you ahead of the game from the get-go.

Of course, you have to investigate to be able to determine if the sellers really know what they are talking about. "Under market" to a property owner may still mean overpriced to you as a real estate investor.

3. Below Appraisal *Below appraisal* is a phrase we like to hear. This occurs when a real estate agent tells us the property they are marketing for the seller is priced below the appraisal value. We know we have the right property and the right seller.

Again, you have to be careful here. Below what appraised value? Are we talking below the appraised value for insurance purposes? Are we talking about the appraised value for property tax purposes? Are we talking about below the appraised value for a home equity loan? Or are we talking about below the appraised value for a recent market comparison? The last value is the only one that counts.

4. Transferred *Transferred* can simply mean *transferred.* Or, transferred can be a code word for an owner in distress. In today's economy, when someone is transferred, they are often happy to have a job to be transferred to.

But they may have been out of a job for a while and be in pre-foreclosure. This is not a pretty sight for the seller. You may be able to put together a very profitable deal.

5. Divorce When you see or hear the word *divorce,* there is often a real estate deal close by. There are 2 to 3 million new marriages each year in the United States. There are 1 to 1.5 million divorces. What happens to the family home when there is a divorce? Statistics tell us that most real estate in a divorce winds up being sold so that the assets can be divided between the ex-spouses.

We have found the best offers in a divorce-involved property are all-cash offers. Each side is willing to take a hit on the purchase price because each wants as much of their equity in cash as possible. Sometimes we have been able to put a deal together several months after the divorce when the property becomes too much for the remaining party to handle.

6. Foreclosure Ad Usually, you see something like this in a real estate classified ad:

Seller in foreclosure.

Bring all offers.

3Br/2Ba $169,500

Good area.

(817) 555-2455

Call on the ad. Identify yourself as a real estate investor. Find out when the foreclosure sale is scheduled to occur. Set an appointment to meet with the owners to show them the foreclosure options presentation. Make an offer to buy their equity.

7. Illness Ad Unfortunately, illness is a fact of life. Sometimes your job as a real estate investor can really help people out of a tough situation. A real estate ad we saw read something like this:

> Illness forces sale.
>
> Great family home in good area.
>
> Priced to sell. $275,000.
>
> Call Jon. (972) 555-2455

We called Jon and found out that his wife had multiple sclerosis. They had a two-story home, and Jon's wife could no longer climb the stairs. They were selling because they needed a one-story home, and they needed money for medical bills. This was a pre-foreclosure waiting to happen.

8. Death "Death forces sale." This was the heading of a classified ad we read one morning in our local newspaper. Pretty tough situation. But the widow needed to sell after her husband was killed in a traffic accident.

The notice of default had already been posted. We made an equity-share offer on the property. We agreed to a price for today and to split any future appreciation 50-50. We would split the monthly payments 50-50. That way she could stay in the property.

9. Owner Will Carry When you see or hear the phrase *owner will carry,* you have found a built-in real estate lender to finance the deal. The owner is going to act as the lender. They are going to carry a mortgage or trust deed for part or all of the purchase price.

We have found that an owner in pre-foreclosure will offer to carry financing in order to make their property more attractive to more buyers. We have asked owners to carry the financing on our equity purchase in order to make the deal work.

10. Nothing Down No down payment. Zero. Nada. *Nothing down* means a seller wants their property to be the most competitive one on the market. This can also be an indication that the owner does not have a lot of time because of an impending foreclosure.

The owner may just want someone to take over the loan payments and get on down the road. Of course, nothing down may just mean nothing down, and you still may be able to make some Quick Cash because of the great terms.

11. 100 Percent Financing A variation of nothing down is *100 percent financing.* We may have a worried seller who has to sell the property and is willing to finance the sale rather than lose all his or her equity. This is one of those phrases that we never pass up when we encounter it.

One thing to look out for when you see "100 percent financing" is a property that will go with VA financing. This means the seller will cooperate with a VA buyer. Although there is no down payment for the VA buyer, this is not seller financing that you can use as a real estate investor.

12. Motivated Seller A *motivated seller* is the right seller. As a real estate investor you are looking for motivated sellers. Sellers in pre-foreclosure are motivated sellers. A motivated seller might just give you the deed to their property and walk away!

It would be fair to say that all the sellers with whom we have done business in the foreclosure arena are motivated. When we encounter sellers who are not motivated, we usually have a very hard time doing business with them.

13. Lost Job/Laid Off The color pink is an anachronism from the twentieth century when people actually got a pink slip to let them know that they were either fired or laid off. In the twenty-first-century economy, companies want fewer workers doing more work.

As a real estate investor, when you see *lost job* or *laid off* in a real estate ad or when one of your personal contacts gives you an alert about someone losing a job, more than likely there is a real estate deal to be made. It is a fact that most people live paycheck to paycheck. When they lose the paycheck, the family home may not be far behind.

Advertise

Sometimes a well-placed advertisement in the newspaper or notices posted on public bulletin boards in supermarkets or business establishments can place an inquisitive owner in contact with you in the pre-foreclosure stage. We have had continuing success with the following verbiage as a newspaper, bulletin board, or Internet ad.

Searching the Public Record

There are two ways to search the public record to glean information about foreclosures or potential foreclosures. You can do it yourself. Or you can pay a foreclosure service to provide you with the foreclosure information.

Do It Yourself For most of you, the public records are at your local county courthouse. For some of you, the public records may be at your city hall. More and more, you can access the public records through the Internet.

The problem with checking the public records yourself is the tremendous amount of records there is to check. That's why title insurance companies have to do a title search on a property before they will issue title insurance. This process can take several weeks. The title insurance company will issue a preliminary title report as a prelude to issuing a policy of title insurance.

We recommend you plan on an entire day to visit the county recorder's office for your county. You will probably find the public records section buried deep in the bowels of your county courthouse.

Ask for Help Ask for help from the staff to direct you to the foreclosure postings for the current month. Once you have the legal description of the property from the foreclosure posting and the property owner's name, you can look up the property in the public record and also check for liens against the owner.

The property record will reflect any liens against the owner. If you are going to do business with a new buyer, you might also want to check the buyer out. For example, if you are going to flip a foreclosure property and carry back financing, this would be a good idea. Sometimes the new buyer will bring clouds to the property title because of liens associated with the buyer personally, like IRS liens.

Brain Trust Divorce is the number-one cause of property foreclosures in this country. A Brain Trust hint for those of you who like being detectives is to follow the public record on filings for dissolution of marriage (the official name for divorce). Then make contact with property owners who are involved with the divorce. This may give you a head start on identifying properties that are headed down the foreclosure path.

Foreclosure Service You can get information about foreclosures from a foreclosure service. A typical price may be $35 a month for the foreclosure list for your county. A typical price for the year may be $225. Shop around because there may be more than one foreclosure service in your area. You don't need anything fancy; just the basic information will do.

We recommend spending the money for a one-month copy. If you decide you like working foreclosures after the notice of default is posted and are going to get into it big time, then pay for six months or a one-year subscription. If this is not the foreclosure phase you are interested in, then you haven't spent too much money for nothing.

Foreclosure Letter For some of you, face-to-face contact with strangers about a subject of such a sensitive nature as foreclosure may prove uncomfortable. Also, it may be tough for property owners facing foreclosure to come to grips with their shame and embarrassment. For both of these reasons, a letter campaign may be a good method to consider in your pursuit of eligible properties.

Although nothing beats personal contact, a program of contacting owners in distress via mail is often the only way of reaching owners who are difficult to find. They may be occupying the property but have an unlisted or disconnected telephone number. They may have vacated the property but left a forwarding address. Just as in the personal contact and telephone meetings, your letter should be honest, sincere, and offer the owner hope.

In addition to the letter, we want you to include a picture of the property, which will create a better impact for the owner. The picture will show the owner that you have a strong interest in the property. After all, you came out to look at the property to take the picture! Make sure you keep a copy of the picture for your files should the property owner contact you at a later date.

The following is the letter we have used. You may want to consider using it. Change it to fit your style and needs. You will notice that this letter is not a short-and-sweet letter. It is a short-and-to-the-point letter. The purpose of your letter is to get the owners' attention—and to have the owner contact you because they feel you can help them.

Dear Property Owner,

According to the public records, the loan on your property may be in trouble. We are writing to you with an offer to help. We are real estate investors who have studied the foreclosure process. We are familiar with the procedure and understand the many ways in which owners can halt the foreclosure and perhaps save their property and equity.

We have made it a practice of contacting owners like yourself who have received official notice of a pending foreclosure. We believe we may be able to help you by providing information about your foreclosure options. Sometimes we find excellent investment opportunities when owners have decided that they no longer wish to keep their property.

Specifically, there are eight actions you can take when your home is in foreclosure. We would like to share these options with you **at no cost or obligation to you.** We do this to increase our chances for investment opportunities and, at the same time, we have an opportunity to help some owners who would otherwise lose their properties.

Time is running out! We urge you to contact us today before any more of your hard-earned equity is lost forever. We can be reached by phone, e-mail, or letter. We will keep our conversation confidential. We hope we can provide you with the information you need to save your property. **DON'T WAIT!** Contact us today!

Chantal and Bill Carey
(817) 555-2614; thetrustee@hotmail.com
P.O. Box 274, Bedford, TX 76095-0274

VA and FHA Foreclosures

You can find out about VA and FHA foreclosures from your local VA and Housing and Urban Development (HUD) offices. They will likely refer you to a list of VA- and FHA-approved real estate brokers in your area who are authorized to list and give access to VA and FHA REOs (real estate-owned properties).

These properties are auctioned off to the highest net bidder. The highest net bidder is the bidder whose bid, after real estate commissions and expenses, generates the most cash to the VA or FHA. Incidentally, your bid must be submitted in writing through an approved real estate broker. These are sealed bids that are opened by the appropriate VA or FHA representatives on a designated date.

Federal National Mortgage Association/Fannie Mae

Fannie Mae (which stands for Federal National Mortgage Association) is a stockholder-owned, congressionally chartered corporation. Its stock is traded on the New York Stock Exchange and other major exchanges. It is listed on the Standard and Poor's 500 Stock Price Index. By buying and selling VA, FHA, and conventional loans in the secondary mortgage market, Fannie Mae is the largest real estate lender in the country.

Fannie Mae Foreclosures Being the largest real estate lender, Fannie Mae has its share of foreclosures. Being a stock corporation, it is profit-oriented and interested in minimizing losses. One method of doing so is the Fannie Mae Pre-Foreclosure Sale program.

The result to real estate investors can be the purchase of property from potential borrowers-in-default at prices below the existing loan and with new loan terms that are better than terms available on the open market. This is done on a case-by-case basis.

Why would Fannie Mae be willing to do this? The answer is to minimize losses. It is expensive for Fannie Mae to foreclose on, maintain, and then remarket a portfolio of properties. If it can dispose of the properties in pre-foreclosure, before it takes them into its property portfolio, Fannie Mae can save money.

In Chapter 11 we will present more information about the Fannie Mae pre-foreclosure program. Suffice it to say here that Fannie Mae is willing to pass on some of the money it saves to real estate investors who purchase property under this program. Some of you are going to make some Quick Cash doing this type of foreclosure investing.

The program is directed toward real estate agents as the contact source with defaulting borrowers, potential retail or wholesale buyers, and the lenders, including Fannie Mae. Just as with the VA and FHA foreclosures, you have to discover who the real estate brokers are who are handling Fannie Mae properties. Whether Fannie Mae moves to a new program, it will always be a source of foreclosure opportunities. Once you have established contact with a Fannie Mae broker, he or she will be able to keep you informed on any changes.

You are now ready to come full circle and learn to negotiate with the owner in the pre-foreclosure time period. In the next chapter we will show you how to present the eight foreclosure options to the owner in distress. This is the beginning of where the rubber meets the road on your journey to making Quick Cash in foreclosures.

CHAPTER 7

Negotiating with the Owner

In this chapter and the next, we will teach you how to negotiate with owners and buy their equity. Once you have contacted an owner who is in the pre-foreclosure phase, either by phone, letter, or in person, and have set up an appointment, your next step is to prepare for a face-to-face negotiating meeting.

After we show you how to prepare for the meeting, we will show you how to make the foreclosure options presentation. Negotiating with the owner then becomes a simple task of helping them choose their best option. Of course, the best option for you is that the owner agrees to sell their property to you. It is important to realize, though, that you may not wind up making a deal right away.

Benefits to the Owner

Many of the foreclosure options benefit just the owner. But we have found that even when we help an owner and don't come away with a deal for us, we still benefit. Many times owners solve their foreclosure problem only temporarily. If they can't resolve the root cause of the problem that led to the foreclosure to begin with, they are likely to wind up in foreclosure again. Our experience is that this occurs 9 times out of 10.

Whom do you think they will call the next time they are in trouble? They will call us (you). We helped them the first time. Maybe we can help them the second time. And if there is nothing they can do to avoid an impending foreclosure sale, whom do you think has the inside track on making a good real estate investment?

Preparation for the Meeting

Obtain All Preliminary Information

Preliminary information includes a copy of the notice of default (if any), a property profile from a title insurance company, and confirmation of property taxes paid or owed. Bring any pictures of the property that you have taken. Bring the comparable sales information you have compiled from a real estate agent or title company.

Include any letters of testimonial you have received from prior transactions. If you also have character letters, bring them, too. Itemize the costs to repair and improve the property to a salable condition. Estimate the costs for holding, marketing, and selling the property. Always include real estate commissions, which can be substantial.

Put together a presentation book, which includes all of this information. Add to it the foreclosure options presentation and questions for the owner. Although you may not use or need all the information at the meeting, we have found it is much better to be overprepared than underprepared.

Questions for the Owner

We recommend you ask and get the answers to the following five questions at the beginning of the meeting. The answers may help you to determine if you should continue on with the meeting or what direction to emphasize during the meeting.

1. Are you aware of the impending foreclosure? You would be surprised at some of the answers we have gotten to this question. Some people stick their head in the sand and want to pretend that everything is going to be all right.

Most people do not know the timeline for the foreclosure process. Some people think they have all the time in the world. We are there to assure them that time is really of the essence for their situation.

2. Do you know what you will have to do to protect your interests? Most people do not have a clue about what they can do to protect their interests in their property. This question introduces the foreclosure options presentation. Some people have a completely mistaken idea of what they can do. Other people are resigned to the fact that there is nothing they can do, even when that isn't true.

3. Are you willing to take the time and effort to fight the foreclosure? When people are facing foreclosure, there may be many other pressing problems occurring at the same time. There may be a job loss or an illness in the family. Just having enough money to buy food and keep the lights on may be a struggle. Having the time, energy, and resources to fight a foreclosure action just may not be possible for them.

4. If we were able to get you cash, would you be willing to sell your equity to us at a discount? This is a testing question. You want the owners to come to grips with the fact that they may have to make a deal. You are also letting them know that you are there as a real estate investor who has to make a profit in order to be able to help them.

5. If you feel comfortable working with us, is there any reason you can see why we couldn't do business? This is a trial closing question. You want the owners to say that if they feel comfortable with you, there is no reason they can see why you couldn't do business. However, the question will also elicit other useful information.

You may discover that the owner is going to deed the property to his brother-in-law for a quick $5,000. The owner is meeting with you because he wants to hear about his foreclosure options besides the brother-in-law route.

Owners may also say that they have an agreement with another investor and want to see if you are going to make them a better offer. Now you know whom your competition is.

At the Meeting

Once we have asked the owners the five questions and gotten their answers, we proceed to the foreclosure options presentation if it is appropriate. We have decided on several occasions to cut short the meeting without making the foreclosure options presentation.

The owners may tell us they will not sell their equity to us at a discount. They may say they already have a deal. They may tell us that they will not do business with us even if they feel comfortable. We may feel we are wasting our time. The point is that you will have to decide whether to stay or go.

Foreclosure Options

There are eight actions the owner can take in response to a notice of default: (1) reinstatement, (2) redemption, (3) deed in lieu of foreclosure, (4) legal delay, (5) bankruptcy, (6) renegotiate with the lender, (7) sell the property, and (8) do nothing. We use the foreclosure options presentation once we are in front of the property owner. We recommend that you put each of these eight options on a separate sheet of paper. We will refer to the Texas and California foreclosure timelines for the time periods to implement these options.

Reinstatement The reinstatement option gives the owner the opportunity to make up back payments plus any incidental charges such a filing or posting notices and trustee service charges. The payment of the reinstatement amount will cancel the foreclosure and enable the borrower to continue as if no default occurred.

In Texas the borrower may reinstate his or her loan within the 20 days from receiving the first official letter from the lender and before receiving the second official letter. Once the borrower receives the second letter from the lender, reinstatement is only possible if the lender agrees to the reinstatement. In the following figure we match the eight foreclosure options with where in the foreclosure timeline they can be done.

Redemption In order to redeem the loan, the borrower must pay off the loan in full. This may be accomplished through refinancing (with a cosigner perhaps) or by a relative or friend bailing out the owner in return for an equity position.

Most states permit redemption up to the foreclosure sale. In California the owner must redeem after they receive the posting at the courthouse and have up to the date of the foreclosure sale, unless the lender agrees to reinstatement.

Texas Foreclosure Timeline

2 – 3 Months	20 Days		Can Be 1 Day	21 Days Minimum
No Payments	1st Official Letter	2nd Official Letter	Posting at Courthouse	Sale 1st Tuesday

1. Reinstatement ______________________

2. ______________ Redemption ______________

3. Deed In Lieu of Foreclosure ______________

4. Legal Delay ______________________

5. File Bankruptcy ______________________

6. Renegotiate ______________________

7. Sell the Property ______________________

8. Do Nothing ______________________

California Foreclosure Timeline

2 – 3 Months	3 – 4 Weeks		3 Months	20 Days	Next Day
No Payments	1st Official Letter	2nd Official Letter	Posting at Courthouse	Redeem Only	Sale

2. ______________ Redemption ______________

Deed in Lieu of Foreclosure For owners who know they will have no opportunity to reinstate, redeem, or even sell their property and just want out of the property, a deed in lieu of foreclosure may be a viable foreclosure alternative. Sometimes the owner can turn the ownership of the property over to the bank and avoid the trauma of foreclosure. This action will reduce the negative impact on the owner's credit. In most states, including Texas, an owner can execute a deed of foreclosure up till the foreclosure sale.

When a lender takes a deed in lieu of foreclosure from a borrower, the lender receives the property subject to all junior and senior liens. This can be potentially hazardous to the lender. The property could be overencumbered with tax liens, judgments, and other involuntary liens. It is most important for the lender to get an up-to-date title report the day the deed is to be accepted.

If the title report shows trouble that the lender doesn't want to deal with, the lender should proceed with the foreclosure sale rather than accept the deed. On the other hand, if the title report shows no other liens but the lender's, the lender may choose to accept the deed.

Caution Additional caution should be taken whenever accepting a deed in lieu of foreclosure. The debtors could later claim that the lender took unfair advantage of them, by offering them no or low compensation for the equity they did have in the property.

The courts have been known to rule in favor of the former property owner and allow the borrower to reclaim the property or cloud the lender's title with a lawsuit. Lenders, to protect themselves, will request a written acknowledgment from the borrower stating that the borrower has received fair consideration for the property. Lenders also have the transaction handled by a title company. That way they have a better chance of getting marketable title.

Legal Delay If the owner can prove that the amount in default is inaccurate, often the owner can delay the foreclosure proceeding and gain additional time to find a more acceptable solution. The maximum time extension is effectively the time it would take to start the foreclosure process over again. The owner may also cause a legal delay up to the foreclosure sale itself. This action is not only possible in California, but in every other state as well.

File Bankruptcy Although this is not a permanent cure, filing bankruptcy can temporarily halt the foreclosure process. Before considering this option, the owner should seek the advice of an attorney. The owner may file bankruptcy up to the day of the foreclosure sale.

Bankruptcy is a serious event that could affect the timing and ultimate outcome of any foreclosure. Bankruptcy is a legal procedure established by federal law to assist debtors who can't meet their financial obligations. The founding fathers of this country were so opposed to the traditional British solution of throwing debtors into prison that they created an alternative solution.

Two Categories Bankruptcies fall into two categories; liquidation and reorganization. Liquidation bankruptcies fall under Chapter 7 of the United States Bankruptcy Code. The debtor who takes this path ends up turning over all his or her nonexempt assets to the bankruptcy court.

A court-appointed trustee then has the responsibility of liquidating (selling) the assets and distributing the proceeds to the existing creditors on a pro rata basis. Any debts that remain unsatisfied at that time are discharged and legally nullified. The trustee works for both the debtor and the creditors. It is the duty of the trustee to try and preserve the debtor's assets as much as possible to satisfy creditors.

Bankruptcies intended to assist the debtor with financial rehabilitation through reorganization come under the categories of Chapter 13 and Chapter 11 of the United States Bankruptcy Code. A Chapter 13 is intended for individuals with a regular source of income. A plan is proposed by which the debtor will continue to make payments on his or her debts and make up back payments with interest. A modified, extended schedule is often used to do this.

A Chapter 11 bankruptcy is used by corporations, partnerships, and those individuals who do not qualify for a Chapter 13 plan. The court procedures can be complex and lengthy.

Foreclosure Stops The moment a property owner in default files a petition for bankruptcy, foreclosure proceedings stop immediately. This results from a legal moratorium called an automatic stay imposed by the bankruptcy court. It prevents creditors from pursuing any legal actions to enforce their claims against a debtor.

If a foreclosure sale is held after a bankruptcy petition has been filed, the foreclosure will be ruled null and void by the bankruptcy judge. A lender must first seek relief from the automatic stay in order to proceed. The Bankruptcy Act states that the court must hear a lender's petition for relief from stay within 30 days. If the court fails to do so, the stay is automatically lifted.

The amount of equity found in the property will affect the judge's decision to grant relief from the stay. If there is significant value in the property being foreclosed, the judge will not grant relief from the automatic stay. The hope is that some of that equity can be used to satisfy other creditors. If there is very little equity in the property, the judge will probably grant a relief from the automatic stay and allow the foreclosing lender to proceed.

Cram Down or Short Sale Lenders are most fearful of the court's authority to impose a cram down or short sale provision. The court can move to modify the terms of the mortgage or trust deed. This could include modifying the payment schedule to help the debtor, or actually reducing the principal amount owed on the mortgage note. The cram down provision can only be used with reorganization types of bankruptcies (Chapters 11 and 13), where the property plays a key role in the reorganization plan.

Debtors have come up with some pretty creative ways to stall foreclosures. Maybe you thought that a person can only file a bankruptcy once every seven years. That is true of Chapter 7 liquidations but not true with Chapters 11 and 13 reorganizations.

The law does not prohibit the act of filing bankruptcy, and it is the filing that brings on the automatic stay. Because of this, a growing number of debtors are using that loophole to further delay the foreclosure process. Many judges are now wise to this trickery and will quickly lift the new stay.

Bankruptcies Filed after a Foreclosure Sale There have been cases reported in which a bankruptcy judge has overturned a foreclosure sale that occurred just prior to the filing of the bankruptcy petition. The judge may rule that the equity in the property could have been used to pay more creditors.

Because the Bankruptcy Code is a federal law, a debtor in any state can file a bankruptcy petition and stop the foreclosure process. If the bankruptcy petition is filed 15 days into the foreclosure, the foreclosure will resume on the 15th day after the automatic stay is lifted. In other words, the lender does not have to go back to the beginning of the foreclosure. They resume the foreclosure from where it already is.

Renegotiate with the Lender The most overlooked of all the foreclosure options an owner has is the opportunity to renegotiate with the lender. The lender does not want the property back, and any effort by the owner to negotiate a plan that will enable the loan to be back in service for the lender's loan portfolio will be looked upon with great favor by the lender.

Generally, the current month's payment plus a portion of the past-due amount will be considered. In Texas and all other states, the borrower can renegotiate with the lender right up to the foreclosure sale.

Sell the Property For the owners who don't care to save their property, or who have no other choice but to let the property go, selling the property may be the smartest choice. This is true even if they have to sell the property at a bargain price.

This is better for the owners than losing their entire equity and damaging their credit at the same time. Your purpose with the foreclosure options presentation is to have them come to the conclusion that selling you their property is their best and most profitable foreclosure option. Owners can try to sell their property right up to the foreclosure sale in Texas and elsewhere throughout the country.

Do Nothing The owners always have the choice of just letting things happen. They will surely lose their hard-earned equity and damage their credit. They can just about forget getting a new home anytime in the foreseeable future.

Unfortunately, we have encountered more than a few people who just put their heads in the sand. They think they are going to win the lottery. They procrastinate until there are no viable options left to prevent the foreclosure sale.

Part of your job as a real estate investor is to motivate the property owner to take action that will benefit the property owner. Doing nothing is a form of action that in this situation has only negative results.

In the next chapter we will show you how to buy the owner's equity. Buying the owner's equity may be different than buying the owner's property. As part of our Quick Cash strategy, you may want to flip the owner's equity to another real estate investor for a fee.

Negotiating with owners becomes more than just buying their equity. You also have to figure out to whom you are going to flip that equity. That person is the source of your Quick Cash. Without a buyer for your good deal, your good deal can turn out not so good.

CHAPTER 8

Buying the Equity

After you have made the foreclosure options presentation, now is the time to ask the owner some additional questions. Your intention is to help the owner make a decision. Since time is really of the essence for them, having the owners make a decision is in their best interest. You are doing them a disservice if you allow them to sell you the "they want to think about it" line.

It has been our experience that when people say they want to think about it, they never do. We have nothing against people thinking. But people use "think about it" as a way to procrastinate. There is no room to procrastinate in the foreclosure arena, especially when you are the person being foreclosed on!

Additional Questions

There are three additional questions that we ask owners.

1. Which of the foreclosure options (from Chapter 7) do the owners think makes the most sense for their situation?

   If they answer with option seven—sell the property—we offer to buy their property. If they answer with anything other than option seven—sell the property—we ask the next question.

2. Do the owners have the time and financial resources to carry out the foreclosure option they think makes the most sense?

   If they cannot answer yes to both the time portion and the financial resources portion of the question, we tell them that that foreclosure option is not going to work. We then offer to buy their property. If they answer yes to both the time and financial resources portions of the question, we ask them the next question.

3. Do the owners want our help in carrying out the foreclosure option they have decided on?

   You have to be careful here. You cannot give the owners legal advice unless you are an attorney. You don't want to get too involved because you open yourself up to liability if things don't work out well for the owners. You also can't waste your time helping them without making any money.

   When the owners say yes, they want our help, we have found that what works best for us is giving them the names of several attorneys who specialize in helping people in foreclosure. We leave the owners our contact information and keep open the possibility that we will buy their property.

   When they say no, they do not want our help, we have found that what works best for us is leaving them our contact information and keeping open the possibility that we will buy their property. In other words, we are flexible knowing they may indeed call us back and offer to sell us their property.

The Owner Wants to Sell You The Property

Let's say you have an owner who wants to sell you the property. What do you offer the owner for the property? You must make your offer based on your analysis of value. Do not make any offers until you read the next section on knowing value.

If you are very comfortable with knowing value in your target area, then you may want to skip ahead to the following section, "Buy the Owner's Equity, Not the Owner's Property." However, we strongly recommend you read this section first. You are an investor buying at a wholesale price. As an investor, you cannot pay a retail price. Make your offer low, and let the owner decide whether to accept.

How do you know that you are buying at a wholesale price? You know you are buying at a wholesale price because you know value. You will become an expert in valuing real estate in your investment target area. You will know the retail value, the wholesale value, the appraised value, the loan value, the replacement value, and the property tax value of every property in which you are investing.

Knowing Value

We are going to take you step by step through the knowledge we have gained as investors valuing real estate. We will define the six values that all real estate investors need to know about the property they are investing in. We will show you the three ways to value real estate that are used by appraisers. We will explain the four elements of value. Then we will reveal four great forces that influence real estate value. Finally, we will teach you seven ways to know value in your target area.

The Six Values Every Real Estate Investor Needs to Know The six values that every real estate investor needs to know are the *retail value,* the *wholesale value,* the *replacement value,* the *property tax value,* the *loan value,* and the *appraised value.* When you know these six values, you can feel confident and comfortable making a real estate investment. When you do not know these six values, you will feel unsure and uncomfortable making a real estate investment.

1. The *retail value* is the value an end user, such as a homeowner, places on a piece of real estate. The retail value tends to be the highest value of all the values placed on real estate.
2. The *wholesale value* is the value a real estate investor like you places on a piece of real estate. The wholesale value tends to be the lowest value of all the values placed on real estate.
3. The *replacement value* is the value insurance companies place on the improvements on a piece of real estate. The replacement value is determined by the cost approach to value.
4. The *property tax value* is the value the local property tax assessor places on a piece of property. The property tax value can be higher or lower than the retail value.
5. The *loan value* is the value a real estate lender places on a piece of real estate. The loan value tends to vary as a percentage of the appraised value.

6. The *appraised value* is the value a real estate appraiser places on a piece of property. The appraised value is typically at or near the retail value.

Three Ways to Value Real Estate There are three ways to value real estate. These are the *cost approach,* the *income approach,* and the *market comparison approach.* These three approaches are the approaches used by professional real estate appraisers when they are appraising a property.

When you understand these three approaches to valuing real estate, you will begin to start thinking like a professional appraiser. As you encounter a property, you will begin to think what approach to value makes the most sense to use with that property.

1. The *cost approach* consists of three parts. First, value the land. Second, value the improvements and add the value of the improvements to the value of the land. Third, determine the accrued depreciation of the improvements and subtract the accrued depreciation from the combined value of the land and improvements.
2. The *income approach* uses the income a property produces to determine its value. We say it this way: The value of an income property is in direct relationship to the income the property produces.
3. The *market comparison approach* uses the value of similar properties to determine the value of a particular property. You compare properties that are similar to the property you are interested in to determine its value. We say it this way: No comparables, no contract.

Four Elements of Value There are four elements of value. These four elements are *demand, utility, scarcity,* and *transferability.* These four elements are the constituent parts of value. We remember these four elements with the acronym DUST: demand, utility, scarcity, and transferability.

When you know the four elements of value, you have an advantage over your competition. You may see a use for a property that no one else sees. You may figure out a way to transfer a property title that other people cannot figure out how to transfer.

1. *Demand* is the number of people who want the property. The more people who want the property, the more valuable it becomes.
2. *Utility* is the use that a property can be put to or made of. The more uses a property can be put to or made of, the more valuable the property.
3. *Scarcity* has to do with the supply of real estate available. This supply could be what is on the market, or it could be the total possible number of properties in the area. The more scarce the supply of real estate available, the more valuable the property.
4. *Transferability* is the key element of value in real estate. You can have the best property in the world, worth millions of dollars, and if you cannot transfer the title to your property, your property becomes worthless. Likewise, if you are a real estate investor and have written a great wholesale offer that has been accepted by the owner, your deal is worthless unless you can get the owner to transfer clear property title to you.

Four Great Forces Influencing Value There are four great forces that influence value. They are *physical forces, economic forces, political forces,* and *social forces.* They are called great forces because they are outside or independent of the property itself. When you understand these four great forces that influence real estate value, you will have a sense of when and how the real estate market can change direction.

1. *Physical forces* are the availability of schools, shopping, churches, transportation, and parks. If these physical amenities are present in your target area, this influences the value of the area in an upward manner. If these physical amenities are not present or are minimally present in your target area, this influences the area in a downward manner.
2. *Economic forces* are the number and types of jobs available, the wages being paid, where in the economic cycle the economy is nationally, and the interest rates for real estate loans. The economic cycle is a repeating expansion-prosperity-recession-depression cycle.

   Real estate value is greatly influenced by the economic cycle. Typically, real estate is said to do well in the expansion and prosperity phases of the economic cycle and poorly in the recession and depression phases of the economic cycle.

3. *Political forces* are the types of zoning, pro-growth or no-growth policies, and environmental regulations. A zoning change can greatly affect the value of a piece of property. It is important for you to know the political forces that influence the value of real estate in your area, for both the present and future investment climates.
4. *Social forces* are the quality of the schools and the number in the area, blighted or well-kept neighborhoods, racial or ethnic strife, and social amenities like museums, art galleries, and concert halls.

Seven Ways to Know Value in Your Target Area There are seven ways to know value in your target area. They include *sold comparables, pending comparables, listed comparables, expired comparables, appreciation rates, new or planned developments,* and *vacancy rates.* The first five of these can be obtained from your local real estate broker. The last two can be obtained from the local planning commission and the apartment owner's association.

1. *Sold comparables* are comparable properties that have been sold and have actually closed escrow. Sold comparables set the floor of retail value for real estate. This means that if a sold comparable had a sell price of $125,000, a similar property should sell no lower than $125,000 in a normal real estate market. Sold comparables are useful for properties that have sold in the last six months. Anything sold beyond six months is not considered a good comparable.
2. *Pending comparables* are properties that have sold but that have not closed escrow. Pending comparables indicate the direction of real estate value. When the pending comparables close escrow, they become sold comparables. If the sold comparables are indicating a value of $125,000 and the pending comparables are indicating a value of $127,000, then you have an indication that the direction of real estate values is going up.
3. *Listed comparables* are properties currently on the market and similar to the property in which you are considering investing. Listed comparables set the ceiling of retail value for

real estate. They set the ceiling because they have neither sold nor closed escrow. They are merely an indicator of what owners would like to get for their properties.

4. *Expired comparables* are properties that never sold, let alone closed escrow. Expired listings indicate the value beyond the present market in terms of what retail real estate buyers are willing to pay for property. Retail buyers will buy the lower-priced comparable properties first, all else being equal.
5. *Appreciation rates* indicate the annual percentage increases in market value. Appreciation rates give you a sense of how hot or cold the real estate market is. Double-digit appreciation rates indicate a hot real estate market. Single-digit rates indicate a good market, and zero or negative rates indicate a cold real estate market.
6. *New or planned developments* indicate the path of development. When you can buy property in the path of that development, you are helping to ensure that you are buying property that will appreciate in value.

   While this may not seem to be important for the Quick Cash strategy, it is. You may very well be flipping the property to an investor who is a long-term wealth builder and who is thus very interested in the property appreciating.
7. *Vacancy rates* indicate an area that may have potential or problems. Low vacancy rates indicate an area that may have profitable properties. High vacancy rates indicate an area that may have problem properties.

   After you discover low vacancy rates or high vacancy rates in your target area, you may want to do some more digging to find out why the vacancy rates are low or high. Do the vacancy rates reflect the historical trend for the area? Or is the area in transition?

Buy the Owner's Equity, Not the Owner's Property

Now that you know how to determine value, let's take the next step. We have a property owner who is in the foreclosure process and wants to sell us the property. What do we want to buy? Do we want to buy the property? Or do we want to buy the equity? We want to buy the owner's equity.

Why don't we want to buy the owner's property? Because we are not interested in buying or owning property! We are interested in making Quick Cash. The property includes too many liabilities, like a loan that is in the forcclosure process.

What Is the Owner's Equity?

The owner's equity is the difference between the value of the owner's property and any monetary liens or encumbrances against the owner's title to the property. If an owner owns a property free and clear, the owner's equity equals the value of the property.

Since the owner we are dealing with is in foreclosure, there is a monetary lien in the form of a mortgage or trust deed against the owner's title to the property. The owner's equity is the value of the property minus the mortgage balance minus the back payments minus any foreclosure expenses that have already accumulated.

In a non-foreclosure situation, if the retail value of the property is $200,000 and the mortgage balance against the property is $140,000, the owner's equity is $60,000.

In a foreclosure situation the value of a property is no longer the retail value. The property may be run-down. The owner does not have the luxury of a normal marketing time to bring in the highest price. In other words, the value of the property is lowered automatically in a foreclosure situation. Let's say the value of the property is now $185,000 to $190,000.

The mortgage lien goes up in a foreclosure situation. The missed payments are added to the remaining balance of the mortgage. If the owner is behind in their payments $10,000, then the mortgage lien is now $150,000.

If the lender has formally initiated the foreclosure process, there are now foreclosure expenses added to the mortgage balance. Now the owner's equity could be substantially reduced. For illustration purposes we will forgo the foreclosure expenses.

Foreclosure Situation		**Non-Foreclosure Situation**	
Foreclosure Value:	$185,000	Retail Value:	$200,000
Mortgage:	$150,000	Mortgage:	$140,000
Owner's Equity:	$ 35,000	Owner's Equity:	$ 60,000

Your Offer

Instead of the owner's equity being $60,000 in the non-foreclosure situation, the owner's equity is $35,000 in the foreclosure situation. The owner has suffered a $25,000 loss in equity.

Please be clear on what we are saying here. The owner has suffered the equity loss. With a new owner back in control of the property, who is not in a foreclosure situation, the value of the property goes back up. When the value of the property goes back up, the owner's equity increases dollar for dollar.

You are going to offer the owner $10,000 for their $35,000 equity. If you keep the property, you are going to have to pay the lender the $10,000 in back payments to stop the foreclosure. Now you will have $20,000 in the property. If you have to make repairs and do fix up, you may have $3,000 to $5,000 more involved.

Then you add in making mortgage payments, property tax payments, and insurance payments. Resale costs could add another $5,000 to $10,000 or more to your investment. When you add this all up your total is $30,000 to $35,000!

Your Offer

Cash to Owner	$10,000
Cash to Lender	$10,000
Repairs and Fix Up	$ 5,000
Carrying and Resale Costs	$10,000
Total Invested	$35,000

This becomes a negotiating tool for you with the owner. Your point with the owner is that the maximum you can offer them is $10,000 cash for their equity. By giving the owner $10,000 for their equity, you will have $35,000 in the property before you make any money!

We have found that when we show owners these types of figures, they are much more amenable to accepting our offer. We are not trying to be mean to them or take advantage of them. We are trying to help them. But we (you) can't help them if we (you) can't make any money. Otherwise, we (you) will be in a foreclosure situation ourselves!

Making Money

Speaking of making money, let's look at the numbers. The mortgage balance is back to $140,000 (actually a little lower because the back payments reduced the principal, but really not worth mentioning). The property restored to retail value is now worth $200,000 (or perhaps a bit more).

If we sell the property to a retail buyer, we will make a $60,000 gross profit minus the $35,000 invested, equaling a $25,000 net profit. That is a 70 percent return perhaps over a three-month to six-month time period. That makes the investment worth the risk.

If we flip the contract to a real estate investor, we will have no cash to the owner, no cash to the lender, no repairs and fix-up costs, and no carrying and resale costs. Do you think it is possible to flip our contract for $5,000 to $10,000? What is the percentage return on our invested money? Did you say infinite?

Making Money

Retail Buyer		*Wholesale Buyer*	
Sales Price:	$200,000	Flip Fee:	$10,000
Mortgage:	$140,000	Mortgage:	0
Gross Profit:	$ 60,000	Gross Profit:	$10,000
Invested Money:	$ 35,000	Invested Money:	0
Net Profit:	$ 25,000	Net Profit:	$10,000

In the next chapter we will show you how to negotiate with the owner's lender. These are negotiations with the lender in the preforeclosure time period. Being successful in these negotiations can benefit you and the owner. The bottom line is the bottom line when you negotiate with the lender. We devote a later chapter (Chapter 17) to negotiating with the lender after the foreclosure sale takes place.

CHAPTER 9

Negotiating with the Lender Pre-Foreclosure

In this chapter we will show you how to negotiate with the owner's lender in the pre-foreclosure time period. This may be before or after you have put an agreement together with the owner to buy the owner's equity. If you are looking for the information on how to negotiate with the lender after the foreclosure sale, please turn to Chapter 17, "Buying from the Lender."

Before we talk about negotiating with the lender, we need to give you some information on how real estate title to property and real estate financing of property interact. Once you have this information, you will better understand where real estate lenders are coming from and how best to negotiate with them.

Real Estate Paperwork

Understanding the paperwork of real estate is critical to your success as a real estate investor. In this chapter we are going to talk about the paperwork involved in the owner's title and lender financing. In the last chapter of the book we will talk about the paperwork necessary for you as a real estate investor to make and close deals.

There are three aspects to the title and lending paperwork. First, there is the paperwork involved on the title side. Second, there is the paperwork involved on the financing side. Finally, there is the paperwork that bridges the title and financing sides and that is known as the security side.

Title Side

On the title side there are two types of deeds used throughout the country to convey the property title from one owner to the next: grant deeds and warranty deeds. To find out which deed is used in your state please see Appendix A.

Grant Deed A *grant deed* is a deed using the word *grant* in the clause that awards ownership. This written document is used by the grantor (seller) to transfer the title of their property to the grantee (buyer). Grant deeds have two implied warranties. One is that the grantor has not previously transferred the title. The other is that the title is free from encumbrances that are not visible to the grantee. This deed also transfers title acquired after delivery of the deed from the seller to the buyer.

Warranty Deed A *warranty deed* is a deed in which the grantor (usually the seller) guarantees the title to the property to be in the condition indicated in the deed. The grantor agrees to protect the grantee (usually the buyer) against all claims to the property made by anyone other than holders of recorded liens (matters of record). A warranty deed gives a warranty to the title holder.

Grant and Warranty Deeds

Grant Deed		Warranty Deed	
Grantor (Seller or Owner)	Grantee (Buyer)	Grantor (Seller or Owner)	Grantee (Buyer)

Financing Side

The paperwork involved on the financing side is the evidence of the debt. The two types of paperwork that are used as evidence of the debt are the promissory note and the mortgage note. This paperwork is used by lenders and borrowers to create a written agreement about the terms and conditions for the real estate loan.

Promissory Note A *promissory note* is the written contract a borrower signs promising to pay back a definite amount of money by a definite future date to a lender. A promissory note has four basic elements: the amount of the note, the interest rate of the note, the term of the note, and the payments, if any, on the note. A promissory note that has no payments till the due date of the note is called a straight note.

Mortgage Note A *mortgage note* is a written contract signed by a borrower in which the borrower agrees to pay back a lender the amount of money the lender loaned the borrower. Similar to a promissory note, a mortgage note specifies the amount of the note, the interest rate of the note, the term of the note, and the payments on the note.

Promissory and Mortgage Notes

Promissory Note		Mortgage Note	
Borrower (Maker of the Note)	Lender (Holder of the Note)	Borrower (Maker of the Note)	Lender (Holder of the Note)

Security Side

The paperwork involved on the security side includes trust deeds and mortgages. They are regarded as security devices for the promissory notes and mortgage notes, respectively. Another way to say this is that the trust deed and mortgages are the collateral for the lender in the event a borrower defaults on the loan.

They become liens against the property title when they are officially recorded at the county recorder's office in the county in which the property that is the security or collateral for the lien is located. To find out which security device is used in your state, please see Appendix B.

Trust Deed A trust deed is a document, used as a security device for a loan on a property, by which the owner transfers bare (naked) legal title with the power of sale to a trustee. This transfer is in effect until the owner totally pays off the loan.

There are three parties to a trust deed: the trustor, the trustee, and the beneficiary. The trustor is the owner/borrower who transfers the bare legal title with a power of sale to the trustee. The trustee is a person who holds the bare legal title to a property without being the actual owner of the property. The trustee has the power of sale for the lender's benefit. The beneficiary is the lender of money on a property used in a trust deed type of loan.

Trust Deed

1. Trustor (Borrower) **2. Trustee (Power of Sale)**

3. Beneficiary (Lender)

Mortgage Contract A mortgage contract is a document, used as a security device for a loan on a property, by which the owner/borrower promises their property as security or collateral without giving up possession of or title to the property.

There are two parties to a mortgage contract. These two parties are the mortgagor and the mortgagee. The mortgagor is the owner/borrower who uses a mortgage contract to borrow money. The mortgagee is the lender of money on a property used in a mortgage contract type of loan.

Mortgage Contract

1. Mortgagor (Borrower) **2. Mortgagee (Lender)**

What It All Means

Foreclosure is possible because of the paperwork of real estate. The relationship of the title paperwork, the financing paperwork, and the security paperwork protects lenders when they loan money to a borrower.

The security paperwork—trust deeds and mortgages—is the bridge between the ownership, or title, side and the finance side. The promissory notes and mortgage notes create the security devices that become liens against the title to the property.

Once you understand the paperwork of real estate, you will be able to negotiate on an equal footing with lenders. All this paperwork comes down to contracts. All contracts come down to this: What does the paperwork say? When you understand what the paperwork says, then you can control what happens to property. See if this next illustration helps clarify the paperwork relationships.

The Paperwork

Title	**Security Devices**	**Finance**
	(The Bridge)	
Grant Deed or	**Trust Deed------------------**	**Promissory Note**
Warranty Deed	**Trustor / Trustee**	
Grantor / Grantee	**Beneficiary**	
(Seller) / (Buyer)	**(Lender)**	
	Mortgage--------------------	**Mortgage Note**
	Mortgagor / Mortgagee	
	(Borrower) / (Lender)	

Negotiating before You Put the Agreement Together

We suggest negotiating with the lender before you have put any agreement together with the owner. That way, you know how the lender is going to behave. This will eliminate any nasty surprises from the lender down the road. You will need the owner's permission to speak with their lender.

While we recommend that you dispose of properties quickly, especially foreclosures, you may have to hold on to a property longer than you planned. One of the most important areas to negotiate is how the lender is going to respond if you buy the owner's equity and want to take over the existing loan. Most real estate loans have a due-on-sale clause and/or a prepayment penalty.

If the lender wants to play hardball, foreclosure proceedings can begin against you if you don't agree with what the lender wants to do with the loan vis-à-vis interest rates, assumption fees, payment amounts, or prepayment penalties. In this section we are going to give you an overview of the due-on-sale clause. We will also show you the difference between an assumable loan and a subject-to loan. And what is a prepayment penalty, anyway?

Due-on-Sale Clause

A due-on-sale clause is a type of acceleration clause in a promissory note, mortgage note, trust deed, or mortgage contract that gives a lender the right to demand all sums owed to be paid immediately if the owner transfers title to the property.

The legality of the due-on-sale clause was argued all the way to the U.S. Supreme Court in the 1980s. To unify all the states under one legal interpretation, Congress passed the Garn-St. Germain lending bill in 1986. Unfortunately, the due-on-sale clause is legal. It is enforced by the lenders.

Assumable Loan An assumable loan is an existing promissory note or mortgage note secured by a trust deed or mortgage contract, respectively, that is kept at the same interest rate and terms as when the original borrower financed the property.

When you assume a loan, you become primarily liable for the payments and any deficiency judgment arising from a loan default. The owner/borrower becomes secondarily liable for the payments and any deficiency judgment.

Remember, a deficiency judgment is a court decision that makes an individual personally liable for the payoff of a remaining amount due because less than the full amount was obtained by foreclosure on the property.

Lenders typically charge an assumption fee for you to assume a loan. They also want you to qualify for the loan as if you were originating a new loan rather than assuming an existing loan.

Subject-To Loan A subject-to loan is an existing loan for which the buyer agrees to take over responsibility for payments under the same terms and conditions as existed when the original borrower financed the property. However, the original borrower remains primarily responsible for any deficiency judgment in the event of a loan default.

The name *subject-to loan* comes from the fact that the buyer takes over the existing loan subject to the same terms and conditions. The interest rate is the same. The monthly payments are the same. Everything about the loan stays the same. There is no lender approval required for you to take over a loan subject-to as there is when you assume a loan.

We say it this way: When you assume a loan, you are entering into a formal agreement with the lender. When you take over a loan subject-to, there is no formal agreement with the lender.

Subject-to loans do not have a due-on-sale clause in their paperwork. Therefore, the lender cannot threaten you with calling the loan "due-on-sale" when you have made a deal with the owner to transfer title. Pre-1988 VA-guaranteed loans and pre-1986 FHA-insured loans are subject-to loans. Also, many privately held owner financing loans may be subject-to loans.

Prepayment Penalty

A prepayment penalty is a fine imposed on a borrower by a lender for early payoff of a loan or any early payoff of a substantial part of the loan. To find out if there is a prepayment penalty on a loan, as with the due-on-sale clause, check the loan documents. Most prepayment penalties lapse once the loan is on the books for five years.

The amount of the prepayment penalty is usually stated as a certain number of months' interest in addition to the amount remaining on the loan as of the payoff date. Prepayment penalties can be six months' interest or more. This can be quite a substantial amount.

What is the prepayment penalty on a loan if the remaining loan balance is $200,000, the annual interest rate is 7 percent, and the prepayment penalty is six months' interest?

Prepayment Penalty

Loan Balance	$200,000
Interest Rate	× 7%
Annual Interest	$ 14,000
6 Months' Interest	$ 7,000

A lender cannot legally enforce receiving a prepayment penalty as a result of a foreclosure sale. The problem for you as a real estate investor is that the prohibition on the lender receiving a prepayment penalty as a result of a foreclosure sale is lifted if you buy the owner's equity in pre-foreclosure.

Whipsaw Effect A lender can have an owner/borrower or, in this case, you, an investor, caught between the due-on-sale clause and the prepayment penalty. As you attempt to help owners out of a foreclosure situation, we have suggested you buy their equity. You may encounter what we call the whipsaw effect with the lender.

If you try to take over the owner's existing loan subject-to and it is not a subject-to loan, the lender can call the loan all due and payable using the due-on-sale clause. If you tell the lender you are going to pay off the loan, and the loan is less than five years old and stipulates a prepayment penalty, you may get stuck paying the prepayment penalty!

Negotiating after You Put the Agreement Together

You may prefer negotiating with the lender after you have put an agreement together with the owner. Some investors find it a waste of time to negotiate with the lender before they have put an agreement together with the owner. After they have gotten their ducks lined up with the lender, they have found that when they go back to the owner, they cannot reach an agreement to buy the owner's equity.

Talking to the Lender

The earlier in the foreclosure process the lender is contacted, the better it is for the borrower. Sometimes a borrower will call the lender and say, "I haven't missed a payment yet, but I am afraid I am about to." Lenders agree that they want to know about a borrower's financial distress well ahead of the borrower missing that first loan payment.

As far as the lender is concerned, this is the perfect time for the owner in distress to call them. A spokeswoman for Fannie Mae puts it this way: "Don't hide from your lender. If you contact your loan servicer, most of the time you will stay in your home." We will have more on Fannie Mae in Chapter 11.

After you receive an owner's permission to talk to his or her lender, we suggest the following approach. Call the lender and identify yourself as a real estate investor who is working with the owner. Find out from the lender exactly where the owner is in the foreclosure process.

It has been our experience that half the time, some type of loan work-out plan is put together. The other half of the time, when a loan work-out plan is not put together, is where you have your opportunity to make Quick Cash in foreclosures.

You want to know two things from the lender: How much time will you have to flip the property? and How much money will it cost to delay the foreclosure sale?

Brain Trust

We want to give you a Brain Trust idea to keep in the back of your mind when you are negotiating with lenders. Ask them if they would consider selling the promissory or mortgage note to you. Of course, you would want to buy it for a substantial discount from the remaining balance on the note. After all, the note may be headed to foreclosure if it is not already in default.

If you do wind up buying the note from the lender, you now have two options. You can work out a deal with the owner for the equity, as before. Or you can proceed with the foreclosure as the lender. Just something to think about. If you want more on this, e-mail us at thetrustee@hotmail.com.

In the next chapter we will get into FHA and VA foreclosures. In fact, the next chapter begins the first of three chapters on dealing with one or another entity of the federal government. The government wants to sell you its foreclosures. They are not good at being in the real estate ownership business.

CHAPTER 10

FHA and VA Foreclosures

In this chapter we will give you information about Federal Housing Administration (FHA) and Veterans Administration (VA) foreclosures. Either one of these areas may be a niche that some of you will find comfortable to make Quick Cash in foreclosures. Remember, the number-one goal for both FHA and VA is to do a loan work-out plan with the borrower.

Foreclosure is their last resort. Once the FHA or VA forecloses, the government is in the real estate business. FHA and VA REOs (real estate-owned properties) have been the inventory that has made many real estate investors a lot of money.

Just remember that both the FHA and the VA are government bureaucracies. The rules can change midstream. But once you develop a relationship with someone on the inside, that relationship can be worth its weight in gold. Be patient if you decide to participate with FHA or VA foreclosures.

FHA

The FHA is the mortgage insurance branch of the U.S. Department of Housing and Urban Development (HUD). Most people in the real estate arena talk about FHA loans rather than HUD loans. Technically, FHA does not make mortgage loans. It provides mortgage insurance to real estate lenders who comply with FHA mortgage insurance loan requirements.

These loans are made at way above the lender-preferred 80 percent loan-to-value ratio. There are FHA loan programs that require as little as a 3 percent down payment on the part of the borrower. The lender is making as much as a 97 percent loan-to-value ratio loan. Talk about the lender wanting some mortgage insurance protection! Essentially, the FHA is the government version of private mortgage insurance (PMI). Let's look at some numbers.

FHA-Insured Loan

Purchase Price	$100,000
Down Payment	$ 3,000
Mortgage Amount	$ 97,000

FHA Borrower Counseling

Because of the amount of exposure the FHA has when it insures real estate loans, it has developed an extensive program to counsel borrowers who are on the verge of defaulting. We present some of this FHA counseling information here, in a question-and-answer format.

We have two purposes in mind. The first is for you to understand how the FHA thinks and operates. It wants to prevent a foreclosure from occurring. Second, we want you to see how the FHA presents its version of foreclosure options. You may glean some valuable information for your own foreclosure options presentation even if you are not dealing with an FHA owner.

Q. What happens when I miss my mortgage payments?

Foreclosure may occur. This is the legal means your lender can use to repossess (take over) your home. When this happens, you must move out of your house. If your property is worth less than the total amount you owe on your mortgage loan, a deficiency judgment could be pursued. If that happens, you may not only lose your home, but you also would owe HUD an additional amount.

Q. What should I do?

1. Do not ignore the letters from your lender. If you are having problems making your payments, call or write to your lender's loss mitigation department without delay. Explain your situation. Be prepared to provide them with financial information, such as your monthly income and expenses. Without this information, they may not be able to help.
2. Stay in your home for now. You may not qualify for assistance if you abandon your property.
3. Contact a HUD-approved housing counseling agency. These agencies are valuable resources. They frequently have information on services and programs offered by government agencies as well as on private and community organizations that can help you. These services are usually free of charge.

Q. What are my alternatives?

You may be considered for the following.

Special Forbearance Your lender may be able to arrange a repayment plan based on your financial situation and may even provide for a temporary reduction or suspension of your payments. You may qualify for this if you have recently experienced a reduction in income or an increase in living expenses. You must furnish information to your lender to show that you would be able to meet the requirements of the new payment plan.

Mortgage Modification You may be able to refinance the debt and/or extend the term of your mortgage loan. This may help you catch up by reducing the monthly payments to a more affordable level. You may qualify if you have recovered from a financial problem and can afford the new payment amount.

Partial Claim Your lender may be able to work with you to obtain a one-time payment from the FHA insurance fund to bring your mortgage current. You may qualify if the following applies:

1. Your loan is at least 4 months delinquent but no more than 12 months delinquent.
2. You are able to begin making full mortgage payments.

When your lender files a partial claim, HUD will pay your lender the amount necessary to bring your mortgage current. You must execute a promissory note, and a lien will be placed on your property until the promissory note is paid in full. The promissory note is interest-free and is due when you pay off the first mortgage or when you sell the property.

Pre-Foreclosure Sale A pre-foreclosure sale will allow you to avoid foreclosure by selling your property for an amount less than the amount necessary to pay off your mortgage loan. You may qualify if the following applies:

1. The loan is at least two months delinquent.
2. You are able to sell your house within three to five months.
3. A new appraisal (that your lender will obtain) shows that the value of your home meets HUD program guidelines.

Deed in Lieu of Foreclosure As a last resort, you may be able to voluntarily give back your property to the lender. This won't save your house, but it is not as damaging to your credit rating as a foreclosure. You can qualify if the following applies:

1. You are in default and don't qualify for any of the other options.
2. Your attempts at selling the house before foreclosure were unsuccessful.
3. You don't have another FHA mortgage in default.

Q. Should I be aware of anything else?

Yes. Beware of scams! Solutions that sound too simple or too good to be true usually are. If you're selling your home without professional guidance, beware of buyers who try to rush you through the process. Unfortunately, there are people who may try to take advantage of your financial difficulty. Be especially alert to equity skimming and phony counseling agencies.

Equity Skimming In this type of scam a buyer approaches you, offering to get you out of financial trouble by promising to pay off your mortgage or give you a sum of money when the property is sold. The buyer may suggest that you move out quickly and deed the property to him or her. The buyer collects rent for a time, does not make any mortgage payments, and allows the lender to foreclose. Remember, signing over your deed to someone else does not necessarily relieve you of your obligation on your loan.

Phony Counseling Agencies Some groups calling themselves counseling agencies may approach you and offer to perform certain services for a fee. These could well be services you could do for yourself for free, such as negotiating a new payment plan with your lender or pursuing a pre-foreclosure sale.

Q. Are there any precautions I can take?

Here are several precautions that should help you avoid being taken by a scam artist.

1. Don't sign any papers you don't fully understand.
2. Make sure you get all promises in writing.
3. Beware of any contract of sale of loan assumption where you are not formally released from liability for your mortgage debt.
4. Check with a lawyer of your mortgage company before entering into any deal involving your home.
5. If you're selling the house yourself to avoid foreclosure, use *How to Sell Your Home Without a Broker* by Bill and Chantal Carey. (Okay, FHA didn't say that. We're just seeing if you are really paying attention.) Seriously, check to see if there are any complaints against the prospective buyer. You can contact your state's attorney general, the state real estate commission, or the local district attorney's consumer fraud unit for this type of information.

VA

We told you that with government entities, the rules can change midstream. As we were writing this book, the Department of Veterans Affairs altered the way it has done business for 50 years.

The VA can actually loan mortgage money to military personnel. This happens in very rural areas where a mortgage lender may not exist. However, the VA predominantly acts as a guarantor of mortgage loans for veterans purchasing homes. It acts as government mortgage insurance for real estate lenders.

The veteran can buy a home with no money down and obtain a mortgage for 100 percent of the purchase price. Talk about the risk to the lender!

VA-Guaranteed Loan

Purchase Price	$100,000
Down Payment	0
Mortgage Amount	$100,000

The Department of Veterans Affairs acquires properties as a result of foreclosures on VA-guaranteed loans. The VA has awarded a contract to Ocwen Federal Bank FSB in Orlando, Florida, to manage, market, and sell these properties. (This is the change.) At this time all VA REO properties have been removed from the market and are accessible only through Ocwen Bank.

Buying VA REOs

Ocwen Federal Bank began listing VA REO properties in early 2004. The properties are listed by local listing agents through local multiple listing services (MLS). A list of properties for sale may also be obtained from Ocwen's Web site at www.ocwen.com/.

If you are interested in buying one of the VA REO properties once it is listed for sale by Ocwen Federal Bank FSB, you should contact a local real estate broker to see the property and make an offer to purchase that property through that real estate broker. No longer will the VA Office of Jurisdiction manage these properties.

Our Experience Our experience buying VA REOs or, as we call them, VA repos, has been positive. At the foreclosure sale the VA tries to get the highest amount possible for these properties. However, because of the 100 percent financing, very often the VA cannot get anyone to outbid its credit bid at the foreclosure sale.

Let's say the VA guarantees a $100,000 loan. Two years go by, and the owner gets into financial trouble. The VA provides counseling but winds up foreclosing. The property is worth $105,000. The owner is $5,000 behind in the six months of payments. The VA bids $105,000 at the foreclosure. No one is going to bid because the property and the bid are the same amount.

VA Foreclosure

Property Value	$105,000
Credit Bid	$105,000
Profit Potential	0

Once the VA has the title to the property, it is going to make deals. Remember, it has guaranteed repayment of the loan to the actual lender. The VA is out $105,000. Any deficit between what it paid the lender and for what it will eventually sell the property for as a repo will be charged to the veteran-borrower.

We bought this property for $77,850. We flipped this property to another real estate investor for $84,000. We made $6,250. The VA went after the borrower for a $27,250 deficiency. Rather than going to court to get a judgment against the veteran, the VA will withhold benefits if it is not paid back.

VA Repo

Flip Price	$84,000
VA Price	$77,850
Profit	$ 6,250

In the next chapter we will give you the information to work with Fannie Mae, Freddie Mac, and FDIC foreclosures. These are properties that are either in the pre-foreclosure time period or are REOs. For some of you this will be your foreclosure investing niche.

CHAPTER 11

Fannie Mae, Freddie Mac, and FDIC Foreclosures

Before we get into the meat of this chapter, we think it is appropriate to give you some background information on the origin of Fannie Mae. Fannie Mae and Freddie Mac have been in the news lately with regard to some of their business practices and risk taking. Apparently, they are making investments that leave them open to substantial losses if interest rates go up. We won't even touch the accounting conversation!

Suffice it to say that without Fannie Mae and Freddie Mac, real estate lending as we know it would not be possible. You may decide to make an investment in Fannie Mae, itself, given that it is a publicly traded company on the New York Stock Exchange.

Secondary Mortgage Market

The secondary mortgage market was created in the 1930s in response to the failure of banks and thrifts during the Great Depression. People would put their money in a bank and receive a passbook in return. The bank would then loan the money from all the passbooks to people in the community to finance things like real estate purchases.

When the depression hit, people panicked and went to the banks to get their money out. Unfortunately, the banks were holding mortgage paper and did not have the liquidity to give all the passbook holders their cash back. That caused many, many banks to fail.

Fannie Mae (the Federal National Mortgage Association) was created to keep liquidity in the banking system. People would still put their money in the banks. The banks would still loan that money out to consumers in the primary mortgage market so they could finance their real estate purchases. The banks would receive mortgage paper from the borrowers in return for the loan proceeds.

Now the banks could turn around and sell the mortgage paper to Fannie Mae for cash. Fannie Mae then packages millions of dollars of mortgage paper and creates a pool of securities that are backed by the mortgages. Fannie Mae then sells these mortgage-backed securities to large institutional investors to get its cash back. Then the cycle repeats.

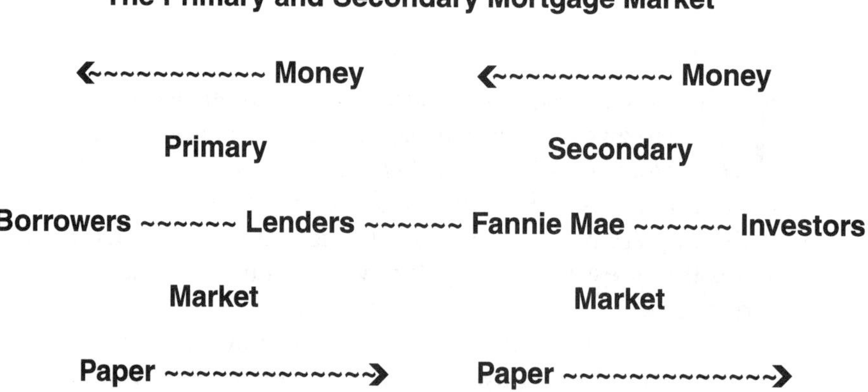

In chapter 6 we told you we would present more information on the Fannie Mae pre-foreclosure sale program. We present it here with a caveat. Just as VA REO rules changed, as we pointed out in the last chapter, Fannie Mae may pull the plug or change the rules on the pre-foreclosure sale program. If Fannie Mae foreclosures are going to be an area you invest in, as with any investment choice, you have to keep yourself informed.

We include in this chapter information on Freddie Mac (Fannie Mae's little brother) and Federal Deposit Insurance Corporation (FDIC) foreclosures. The FDIC is the parent of the Resolution Trust Corporation (RTC), which handled the savings-and-loan debacle of the 1990s. Every one of these entities wants to be a lender for and not an owner of real estate. They want to make a deal with you. Be patient. If you don't like the numbers, move on to another deal.

The Fannie Mae Pre-Foreclosure Sale Program

Fannie Mae is willing to pursue a pre-foreclosure sale at any time prior to the actual foreclosure. It will do this if Fannie Mae's acquisition of the property is the most likely situation at the foreclosure sale. Fannie Mae will proceed with the pre-foreclosure sale if the proceeds of the sale, along with the mortgage insurance settlement, will make them whole or result in a loss less than the one incurred if the property is acquired as an REO.

The Listing Broker's Responsibilities

Once the borrower/owner has worked with the servicing lender and Fannie Mae to determine that he or she is eligible for a pre-foreclosure sale, the borrower/owner will select a listing broker and execute a listing agreement. All parts of the listing agreement are between the broker and the borrower/owner and are not negotiated by the servicing lender or Fannie Mae.

Fannie Mae encourages borrowers to enter into a standard listing agreement that provides for payment of prevailing commissions; however, it cannot dictate what that agreement will be. Also, it cannot direct borrower/owners to use a certain real estate broker, although a list of brokers will be provided by Fannie Mae.

Fannie Mae recommends that the listing broker be prepared to distribute the submission package (detailed in the next section) and earnest money agreement to all involved institutions concurrently. These include the servicing lender, the mortgage insurance company (where applicable), and Fannie Mae.

The submission of the information to all institutions at one time will assist in expediting the acceptance and approval process. However, the listing agent's direct contact must always be with the borrower and the servicing lender. The listing broker should provide any assistance necessary to the borrower/owner in the preparation of the complete submission package.

Submission Package

The submission package should include the borrower's letter of hardship, current financial statement, current pay stub, and the prior year's tax return. If the borrower is self-employed, Fannie Mae will need a copy of a year-to-date profit-and-loss statement, all schedules to the tax return, and a copy of any partnership or corporate tax returns, if applicable.

When Fannie Mae receives the complete submission package, it will coordinate with the servicing lender its recommendation and all pertinent loan detail information. Fannie Mae will also coordinate with the mortgage insurance company to determine any pre-claim settlement agreement and negotiate the mitigation of its loss.

Once all the information has been received, Fannie Mae will coordinate with all parties through the servicing lender any requirements for the borrower to participate in the reduction of any potential loss to Fannie Mae.

Earnest Money Agreements

Any earnest money agreements requiring repairs or maintenance to the property that the borrower/owner cannot financially afford to complete must be explained. Two written bids must be submitted with the agreement to Fannie Mae for their inclusion in the short payoff. (A short payoff is the same as a cram down.)

When Fannie Mae has received an agreement on the proposed preforeclosure sale, it will provide in writing to the servicing lender its approval and authorization for a short payoff. It should be pointed out that Fannie Mae does not actively negotiate or sign any of the purchase agreements. Fannie Mae can only agree to the amount of the loss it will approve. Its intention is to make it as easy as possible for the buying public (that means real estate investors as well as home buyers) and real estate professionals to deal with Fannie Mae.

Questions Most Often Asked by Listing Brokers

If I have been requested to list a home that is in foreclosure, to whom do I present the offer? The initial offer on the property must be made to the borrower, who is the owner of the property. The borrower is the seller and must negotiate as such. The earnest money agreement must then be presented, in copy form, to the servicing lender, Fannie Mae, and the mortgage insurer (if applicable), concurrently.

Do I need to submit anything else with the earnest money agreement? No. There are additional items that will be requested from the seller of the property, which could be facilitated by your assistance. Coordinating the distribution of these items can only help expedite the decision-making process. These items include the borrower's financial statements, tax returns to include all schedules, partnership, and corporation returns, if applicable, hardship letter and supportive documentation, copies of the listing agreement, and any change addendums.

What other information does Fannie Mae need? Fannie Mae will request copies of the current payoff statement, collection records, payment history, mortgage insurance information, and the origination documents from the servicing lender. This would also include the original mortgage application package and appraisal.

The servicing lender is also responsible for ordering two independent brokers' price opinions. The set must be ordered from two separate sources that are not involved in the listing or sale of the property.

Who will be my contact person during the offer review period? All contact must be made with the servicing lender. Fannie Mae's decision and any loss mitigation will be done through this contact person only. The reason is simple. It is counterproductive for all parties if the listing and selling agents and the seller and buyer are all calling the lender, the mortgage insurer, and Fannie Mae for the current status of the loss review.

If the pre-foreclosure sale submission is distributed in its complete form to all parties concurrently, you can expect a response within two to three weeks. Please allow for this amount of time in your agreements.

Is there a preset limit of the closing costs or discount points Fannie Mae will pay? No. Conventional seller percentage closing costs will be considered in the loss review.

How do I handle repairs that the purchaser wants? All repairs as listed in the earnest money agreement must be presented with two separate specific bids for the items in need of repair. If necessary, these items may be presented and negotiated with the servicing lender and the homeowner's insurance company.

Will Fannie Mae consider a sale on an investment property? All pre-foreclosure offers will be taken under consideration. Whether Fannie Mae will participate in the acceptance of the short payoff will be based on the review of the circumstances in the request. Other remedies may be available that have not been reviewed or explored with the borrower. Fannie Mae's staff can give you more information on remedies involving investment properties.

On what factors does Fannie Mae base its loss evaluation? Several items are taken into consideration regarding the acceptance of a loss. The original appraisal and two current brokers' price opinions are a part of the evaluation that is done. As mentioned previously, the additional information that is evaluated would be the original mortgage application and the borrower's current financial situation.

Is it worth my time and effort if the property is scheduled for foreclosure within the next few weeks, months, and so on? Yes, it is possible to postpone a foreclosure sale that is scheduled to be conducted if there is an active listing and offers are pending. It is worth all efforts to give borrowers with qualifying hardships all the assistance possible.

Fannie Mae Home Saver Solutions Program

Another loan work-out option used by Fannie Mae is the Home Saver Solutions Program. Since starting this program in 1997, Fannie Mae has spent more than $25 million in work-out incentive fees to lenders from whom it has purchased mortgages.

Fannie Mae pays its lender service providers $500 each time they arrange a deed in lieu of foreclosure. They pay $1,000 each time they arrange a pre-foreclosure sale! Are some of you getting any ideas on how to make some Quick Cash here?

Both of these solutions require the homeowners to move out of the property, but their credit rating will not reflect a foreclosure. Fannie Mae also recommends that its lenders use two other approaches. Both allow the homeowners to keep their property. The first is a repayment plan. The second is loan modification.

Repayment plans generally work when the homeowner is just one month behind. The missed payment is added in increments into future regular monthly mortgage payments.

Loan modifications can be arranged for borrowers who can't afford repayment plans. The loan servicer changes the terms of the loan to make it affordable. Variations include lowering the interest rate. Sometimes past-due amounts will be rolled into an extension of the time of the loan.

Fannie Mae has shown a substantial increase in loan work-outs since the program began. The percentage of loans worked out has grown from 35 percent in 1997 to 50 percent in 2003. In real numbers this translates into 26,775 loans worked out; 26,788 properties were foreclosed.

Freddie Mac

The formal name of Freddie Mac is the Federal Home Loan Mortgage Corporation. Freddie Mac is a stockholder-owned corporation chartered by Congress in 1970 to keep money flowing to mortgage lenders in support of homeownership and rental housing.

Freddie Mac purchases single-family and multifamily residential mortgages and mortgage-related securities, which it finances primarily by issuing mortgage pass through securities and debt instruments in the capital markets. By doing so, Freddie Mac ultimately helps homeowners and renters get lower housing costs and better access to home financing.

Properties for Sale

HomeSteps is the second-largest owner/seller of single-family residential real estate in the United States (Fannie Mae is the largest). It is a service brand of Freddie Mac and a free-of-charge service available to home buyers and real estate professionals. HomeSteps handles Freddie Mac's REOs.

When you visit Freddie Mac's Web site (www.freddiemac.com/), you can search the database of homes for sale. Freddie Mac has special financing programs. You can also search the database for a local real estate agent.

FDIC

The FDIC insures the accounts of customers of banks up to $100,000. It is part of the federal government. If a bank becomes insolvent, the FDIC takes over the bank and any of its assets, including the bank's REOs. The FDIC lists these properties on its Web site, www.fdic.gov/.

The FDIC is another resource for making Quick Cash in foreclosures. The FDIC also has service centers called field operations branches in major cities. They have real people that will answer questions concerning FDIC property sales that are not answered on its Web site.

We include here some of the questions and answers from the FDIC Web site to give you a feel for how it does business.

How should I use your listing of properties? This listing of real estate is intended to provide interested parties with preliminary information only. This list is not a solicitation of offers and does not constitute an offer to sell. The information is provided for the purpose of inviting further inquiry and has been obtained from sources we believe to be reliable.

How do I find out more information relating to these properties? Each property will have a contact name and phone number. The contact name will either be an individual from an FDIC office or an individual associated with the sales initiative (e.g., Auction Company, Real Estate Broker). If a property information package (PIP) has been prepared on a particular property, it can be obtained from this individual.

How often is this listing of properties updated? It is the FDIC's intent to update the listing of properties by close of business each Monday. Therefore, with the volatile nature of the real estate business, it is important to find out if the property is still available since the last update.

What is the condition of properties sold by the FDIC? All properties are sold in an *as is* condition. The FDIC makes no guarantee, warranty, or representation, expressed or implied as to the location, quality, kind, character, size, description, or fitness for any use or purpose, now or hereafter. (We think this is the best definition of *as is* condition for real estate we have ever seen. Leave it to the government to make sure it cannot be held responsible.)

How is the listed price established? Listed prices are established by a variety of factors, which may include independent appraisals, brokers' opinions of value, and current market conditions. All prices are subject to change without notice.

Is seller financing available on the properties? Seller financing may be available to qualified buyers on residential properties with a minimum purchase price of $500,000 or those sold as affordable housing and on all commercial and land properties, regardless of price. Specific sale terms and conditions can be obtained from the individual assigned to market the property.

Once an offer is submitted on a property, how is my offer evaluated? A number of criteria are considered when evaluating offers from prospective purchasers. These include, but are not limited to, net funds received after deducting brokerage commissions and sales expenses, and payment terms considered in light of the applicant's creditworthiness and ability to perform. The FDIC reserves the right to accept, reject, or counter any submitted offer. While reviewing such offers, the FDIC further reserves the right to continue its sales efforts, including responding to any inquires or offers to purchase the property.

How can I have my name added to the FDIC real estate mailing list? The FDIC does not maintain a mailing list of those interested in purchasing real estate as the corporation sees the Internet as the most efficient method to communicate its current property listings in a timely fashion. Auctions and Sealed Bid Sales announcements will both appear on the Internet, under the National Asset Sales Calendar-Real Estate Sales, and be advertised in local and regional newspapers.

In the next chapter we will teach you the intricacies of IRS foreclosures. This is a fairly tricky area. You must know about the IRS even if you are not buying foreclosures from them. The IRS has special rights and privileges with regard to foreclosures in general.

If the IRS has a tax lien on a property, you need to find out about it and deal with it. Otherwise, you may be in for a nasty surprise down the road long after you think you have clear title to that foreclosure you picked up four months ago on the courthouse steps.

CHAPTER 12

IRS Foreclosures

The IRS is the biggest business in the world. It is in the cash-flow business. It prefers dealing with liquid assets—money. When it has to take hard assets like real estate from taxpayers in lieu of money for unpaid taxes, it becomes similar to a lender. The IRS does not want to own property. It wants to dispose of property and get the cash.

This creates foreclosure investment opportunities for you. We want you to pay particular attention to the nature of the title the IRS will provide, the form of payment it will accept, and the redemption rights of the taxpayer. Also, notice how the IRS has the right to void the foreclosure sale when it is the junior lien holder against the owner's title. The IRS will do this if it thinks it can resell the property for a higher amount of money.

Cold, hard cash is the name of the game with IRS foreclosures. The IRS is not like a lender who forecloses on a loan and may be willing to finance your acquisition of the foreclosed property. We say it this way: "You have to bring the dough; otherwise don't go."

To be fair, as you will see in the actual IRS examples we will share, it will accept a 20 percent down payment within two hours of you making a winning bid. You just have to come up with the balance within 30 days, or it will keep your deposit! And if the IRS doesn't think it is getting enough money, even if you are the winning bidder, it can void the sale.

IRS Tax Liens

An IRS tax lien gets recorded against all of the taxpayer's property. It can be a junior lien or a senior lien in relationship to other liens against the property. The tax lien travels with the taxpayer and attaches to any new property he or she acquires, whether it is real or personal property.

Just remember a famous musician's IRS problems from about 10 years ago. He took his favorite guitar to one of his houses in Hawaii and hid it in the jungle in back of the property so the IRS wouldn't seize it!

Junior Lien

If the tax lien is a junior lien to the foreclosure, the IRS must be notified by the foreclosing entity. The IRS has the right to sell the property again within 120 days of the foreclosure sale to generate additional funds to pay off the tax lien.

Let's look at some numbers. Let's say the taxpayer's lender is foreclosing on a $140,000 first mortgage. The taxpayer is behind in loan payments in the amount of $10,000. The property has been appraised at $210,000.

Value and Back Payments

Property Value	$210,000
First Mortgage	$140,000
Back Payments	$ 10,000

In the normal foreclosure scenario at the foreclosure sale the lender would make a credit bid of $150,000. This is the combination of the $140,000 first mortgage and the $10,000 in back payments.

Credit Bid

First Mortgage	$140,000
Back Payments	$ 10,000
Credit Bid	$150,000

If you are the winning bidder with a bid of $160,000, you may just have made some Quick Cash in foreclosures.

Quick Cash

Property Value	$210,000
Winning Bid	$160,000
Quick Cash Potential	$ 50,000

What happens if the IRS records a $20,000 tax lien against the owner of the property during the foreclosure process? Same scenario as above, but the lender does not inform the IRS of the foreclosure sale.

The lender holds a senior lien to the IRS lien. Senior liens are liens that have been recorded against the property title before other liens that are recorded against the property title. It is not the size of the lien that makes it senior. It is the earlier recording date that makes it senior. So, in this case, the IRS has a junior lien.

You do not investigate the title past the lien of the lender who is foreclosing. You discover it is the senior lien on the property. You make the $160,000 winning bid. The lender gives you a trustee's deed transferring title to the property to you.

What we know about foreclosures is that when a senior lien holder forecloses, any and all junior liens are extinguished or wiped out. So you think everything is fine. But when the junior lien is an IRS tax lien, it is not wiped out.

Sixty days goes by. You are contacted by the IRS as the owner of the property.

It informs you that it is going to conduct another sale of the property. The IRS knows that the property is worth over $200,000. It thinks it will be able to get some, if not all, of the $20,000 owed to the IRS by the taxpayer.

The property is worth over $200,000 now because in the 60 days that you have owned it, you put $6,000 in repairs and fix up into the property. The IRS conducts another sale. You are welcome to bid again. The IRS will make a credit bid of $180,000.

You see, the IRS must pay back the investor for the money the investor paid at the first foreclosure sale. Because you paid $160,000 at the foreclosure sale, the IRS has to get enough at its sale to pay you plus, it hopes, get the $20,000 it is owed on the tax lien. As far as your $6,000 in repairs and fix up is concerned, too bad! The smart thing to do is not to do any fix up or improvements to the property until the 120 days has passed.

IRS Resale

Investor Payoff	$160,000
Tax Lien	$ 20,000
IRS Credit Bid	$180,000

What happens if someone bids $180,001? The IRS gets $20,000. You get $160,001. Are you seeing something smart for you to do here? Bid! Bid at least $186,000. That way you protect your $6,000 in repairs and fix-up expenses.

If you are so shaken by this whole IRS resale and just want to get out, you hope someone will bid $186,001.

IRS Resale

Winning Bid	$186,001
Tax Lien	$ 20,000
Money to You	$166,001

Last piece. What if your $186,000 bid was the winning bid? You would have to pay the IRS $20,000 to have it release the lien from your property. A hard lesson to learn, but you still may come out with a nice profit if you can flip the property for over $200,000. Let's say you can get $201,000 at a C.Y.A. sale (just think about it for a second).

You would get back the $160,000 you paid at the foreclosure sale to the lender. You would get back the $20,000 you paid IRS. You would get back the $6,000 in repairs and fix-up. You would make a $15,000 profit. How many gray hairs did you say you got on this deal?

C.Y.A. Sale

Purchase Price	$201,000
Foreclosure Price	$160,000
IRS Lien	$ 20,000
Repairs and Fix-Up	$ 6,000
Profit	$ 15,000

Senior Lien

If the tax lien is senior to the foreclosing lender, the buyer at the foreclosure sale takes title to the property subject to the existing IRS tax lien. It may be difficult to receive marketable title to the property for resale while the tax lien remains on the property.

Sometimes the buyer of the foreclosure can negotiate with the IRS. By paying part of the tax lien amount, the IRS may remove the entire lien. The IRS tax liens cloud the property title, which affects transferability of the title. If you can't transfer title, it makes a property very difficult, if not impossible, to sell.

We are going to share with you three types of IRS foreclosures. All three are in the form of public auctions. The first is a public auction conducted by the IRS that looks very similar to a foreclosure auction. The second is a mail-in bid for public auction, also conducted by the IRS. This is similar to an FHA or VA bid process. The third is an IRS judicial auction conducted under the auspices of a U.S. District Court as a civil action.

NOTICE OF PUBLIC AUCTION SALE

Under authority of Internal Revenue Code 6331, the property described here has been seized for nonpayment of internal revenue taxes. The property will be sold at public auction as provided by Internal Revenue Code 6335 and related regulations.

Date June 15, 2005
Time 10:00 A.M.
Sale Location South end of the courthouse steps

Nature of Title
The right, title, and interest of the taxpayer in and to the property is offered for sale subject to any prior valid outstanding mortgages, encumbrances, or other liens in favor of third parties against the taxpayer that are superior to the lien of the United States.

All property is offered for sale where is and as is and without recourse against the United States. No guaranty or condition of any of the property, or its fitness for any use or purpose. No claim will be considered for allowance or adjustment or for rescission of the sale based on failure of the property to conform with any expressed or implied representation.

Description of Property ______________________________
Property May Be Inspected At ___________________________

The Terms of Payment
20% of highest bid due within two hours from auction conclusion and balance paid in full within 30 days from auction.

Form of Payment
All payment must be by cash, certified, cashier's or treasurer's check drawn on any bank or trust company incorporated under the laws of the United States. Payment may also be made by any United State Postal, bank, express or telegraph money order. Make check or money order payable to the United States Treasury.

Additional Information
If you want additional information about the property and proposed sale, please contact the office at the address below.

Mary Beth Justice
Property Appraisal & Liquidation Specialist
Address
Phone Fax

Mary Beth Justice is the IRS version of a combination real estate broker and lender's REO manager. Let's take a look at the second IRS foreclosure. The mail-in bid may be done for properties located in remote locations.

MAIL-IN BID FOR PUBLIC AUCTION SALE

I, the undersigned, bid $__________ on ____________ offered for sale by public auction on _______. I enclose my payment of $_____, which is 20% of my bid and authorize the enclosed payment to be applied against the sale price if I am the successful bidder.

I understand that this mail-in bid must be received at the address below by ___________________ to be included in the sale, with the balance due to be paid in full no later than________________. **Note:** The form of payment and/or bid must comply with the Terms of Payment as stated on the Notice of Public Auction Sale.

Bidder's Name (Print) ________________________________
Bidder's Phone Number ______________________________
Bidder's Address ____________________________________
____

By submitting this mail-in bid, I understand that:
This is a mail-in bid for a public auction sale, and it is not a sealed bid sale; I must comply with all other conditions as stated in the Notice of Public Auction Sale.

There are advantages that I am forgoing by not being present at the actual sale, such as inspecting the property, hearing any statement by the taxpayer or lien holders, and engaging in open, competitive bidding.

Signature of Bidder ______________________________

Submit the bid in a securely sealed envelope with your name, address, and date of the sale on the upper left corner of the envelope. Address to submit MAIL-IN BID and Deposit.

Mary Beth Justice
Property Appraisal & Liquidation Specialist
Internal Revenue Service
Address

Annotate the envelope with the following statement. MAIL-IN BID—TO BE OPENED BY PALS (Property Appraisal & Liquidation Specialist) ONLY.

Before we get to the third IRS foreclosure, we are going to present the IRS redemption rights for the property owner. These rights are different than the IRS's right to void a foreclosure sale within 120 days in order to resell the property to get more money.

REDEMPTION RIGHTS

The rights of redemption, as specified in Internal Revenue Code section 6337, are quoted as follows:

Section 6337. Redemption of Property.

(a) Before Sale.—Any person whose property has been levied upon shall have the right to pay the amount due, together with the expenses of the proceeding, if any, to the Secretary at any time prior to the sale thereof, and upon such payment the Secretary shall restore such property to him, and all further proceedings in connection with the levy on such property shall cease from the time of such payment.

(b) Redemption of Real Estate After Sale.

(1) Period.—the owners of any real property sold as provided in section 6335, their heirs, executors, or administrators, or any person having an interest therein, or a lien thereon, or any person in their behalf, shall be permitted to redeem the property sold, or any particular tract of such property at any time within 180 days after the sale thereof.

(2) Price.—Such property or tract of property shall be permitted to be redeemed upon payment to the purchaser, or in case he cannot be found in the county in which the property to be redeemed is situated, then to the Secretary, for the use of the purchaser, his heirs, or assigns, the amount paid by such purchaser and interest thereon at the rate of 20 percent per annum.

Section 6339 (c). Effect of Junior Encumbrances.

A certificate of sale of personal property given or a deed to real property executed pursuant to section 6338 shall discharge such property from all liens, encumbrances, and titles over which the lien of the United States with respect to which the levy was made had priority.

Form of payment

All payments must be by cash, certified check, cashier's or treasurer's check or by United States postal, bank, express, or telegraph money order. Make a check or money order payable to the Internal Revenue Service or U.S. Treasury Department.

IRS AUCTION—JUDICIAL

Pursuant to 28 U.S.C. Sections 2001 and 2002, an Order of Sale entered in United States v. The Taxpayer, et al., Civil No__________; the United States will offer to sell at public auction, property located at

____

____

Date & Time
Sale Location
Minimum Bid
Description of Property
Terms and Conditions of Sale

At the time of sale, the successful bidder shall be required to deposit at least 10% of the amount of the bid; made by cash, certified or cashier's check payable to: Clerk of the United States District Court for the_________________________. Before being permitted to bid at the sale, bidders shall display to the Internal Revenue Service proof that they are able to comply with this requirement. No bids will be accepted from anyone who has not presented that proof.

The balance of the purchase price for the realty is to be paid to the Internal Revenue Service, Property Appraisal and Liquidation Specialist, within 60 days after the bid is accepted by certified or cashier's check payable to : Clerk of the United States District Court for the _________________________. If the bidder fails to fulfill this requirement, the deposit shall be forfeited and shall be applied to the expenses of sale, with any amount remaining returned to the bidder. The realty shall again be offered for sale, under the terms and conditions of the judgment and decree.

The real property shall be sold to the highest bidder with the United States having the right to withdraw the property from bidding at any time prior to the acceptance of a bid, if in the United States' opinion, the bids are inadequate. The said real estate shall be sold free and clear of the federal tax liens, and free of all claims, if any, of the parties to this action.

Satisfaction of any municipal tax liens shall be from the sale proceeds, and the properties shall be sold free and clear of such municipal liens. The sale shall be subject to building lines if established, all laws, ordinances, and governmental regulation (including building and zoning ordinances), affecting the premises, and easements of record, if any.

Upon the sale of the property, all persons, if any, occupying that real property shall permanently leave and vacate the premises taking with them their personal property (but leaving all buildings, fixtures, and improvements to the realty).

The property is offered for sale as is and where is and without recourse against the United States. The United States makes no guarantee of condition of the property, or its fitness for any purpose. The United States will not consider any claim for allowance or adjustment or for the rescission of the sale based on failure of the property to comply with any expressed or implied representation.

The sale of the real property shall be subject to confirmation by the U.S. District Court for the _________________________. On confirmation of the sale, all interests in, liens against, or claims to, the real property that are held or asserted by the United States or any of the defendants in Civil No.________ will be discharged or extinguished. On confirmation of the sale, a deed of judicial sale conveying the real property to the purchase shall be delivered.

Important Information
This is not an advertisement for the sale of seized property. Instead, this notice contains information regarding the procedures for the sale of foreclosed property under the auspices of the U.S. District Court in Civil No. ______. The information stated in other hyperlinks on the web page does not apply to this type of sale.

Summary

The IRS property auctions Web site is located at www.treas.gov/auctions/irs/realty. Now that we have given you all the information on where to find foreclosures, who conducts foreclosures, and how to buy foreclosures, it is time to show you how to make Quick Cash in foreclosures.

In the next chapter we will finally arrive on the courthouse steps. This is the phase of the foreclosure process that most people think is the only time period you can invest in foreclosures—at the foreclosure sale itself. This may be the worst time to invest in the foreclosure market. But we shall see.

CHAPTER 13

Buying on the Courthouse Steps

For those of you who wait until the day of the foreclosure sale to go after a foreclosure investment opportunity, preparation is of utmost importance. The bidding on the courthouse steps is often fast-paced, and you will have little time to make a decision. This may mean a poor outcome if you have not already inspected the property and made a title evaluation.

You need to come prepared in the financing department, too. Cash or cashier's checks are all that will be accepted by the trustee, sheriff, or other representative of the foreclosing party. You have to strike a balance between bringing enough to win the bid and not bringing too much so that you go overboard and make a stupid purchase.

Gathering Information before You Bid

To assist an investor in getting the information about a property prior to bidding there are two reports: a lot book report and a judgment lien report. Check with your local title insurance company for their availability in your area.

They are the most economical way of getting information about liens against the property short of getting a preliminary title report, which will cost you more. A property profile will not give you that information, and you would be foolish to rely on a property profile alone.

Lot Book Report

The lot book report contains a record of everything that has been recorded against the property. Every property has a lien for property taxes. This is true even when the property taxes have been paid and the property tax account is current. Property taxes create a lien against the title to the property, which is called a lien that is due and not yet payable.

Any trust deeds or mortgages, which are the security devices for promissory notes or mortgage notes, respectively, and have been recorded against the property title can be found in the lot book report. Also, any other liens or encumbrances that affect the title such as easements will show up.

Judgment Lien Report

The judgment lien report contains a record of any money judgments that have been recorded against the owner of record for the property. These can include IRS liens, civil lawsuit judgments, state income tax liens, personal property taxes, and family court matters.

You can go down to the county courthouse to research the recorded liens yourself, if you know where to look and what to look for. Ask for help from the clerks. They will usually be glad to oblige. We recommend you do this at least one time so you get a sense of the huge amount of materials that are recorded.

Why this information is important becomes apparent if you ignore it. Remember, when you are the winning bidder at the foreclosure sale and get title to the property from the foreclosing entity, you get the title subject to all the senior liens and encumbrances.

When we talked about knowing value, we said that transferability was a critical element of value. You are the winning bidder and proud owner of the title to a property. You have nothing if you cannot transfer clear ownership title to another buyer.

Dry Run

To gain the greatest advantage at the foreclosure sale, we recommend you do a dry run by attending one or two sales on property you are not interested in prior to the sale of the property you are interested in. This rehearsal will help give you the confidence you need to be successful at foreclosure sales.

Your observation of a foreclosure sale will be even more useful if you can witness a sale conducted by the same trustee, sheriff, or representative of the foreclosing party as the one that will conduct the foreclosure sale on the property or properties that you are interested in.

How Foreclosure Sales Are Conducted

There are minor differences in the manner in which foreclosure sales are conducted throughout the country. Your mission is to find out everything about the foreclosure sales in your neck of the woods. For purposes of illustration, we will use the Trustee's Sales in California as our guide.

Trustee's Sales in California

According to regulation, Trustee's Sales in California are held between 9:00 A.M. and 5:00 P.M. weekdays and may be held at any public place. Although many are held on the courthouse steps, the proximity to the courthouse is of little importance.

In fact, some lenders who want to discourage other people from bidding (usually private lenders who want to take the property back) will often schedule the foreclosure sale at some remote location in the county where the property is located just to keep away the competition.

Julian, California We attended a foreclosure sale in Julian, California, for a property located in the city of San Diego. Julian is more than 50 miles from San Diego but is in the same county. Needless to say, not many people were at the foreclosure sale.

But that was the point. The holder of a second trust deed was foreclosing. He wanted to make the credit bid and get title to the property. If no one else came to the foreclosure sale, he would wind up winning the bid. There was a small first trust deed on the property, and it was a low loan-to-value ratio.

As a foreclosing second trust deed holder, he could step in and take over the first trust deed by just making the payments. There was almost a $100,000 equity position for the holder of the second if they could acquire the property in this manner. Unfortunately for him, we had done our homework and knew what was going on.

Who Conducts the Foreclosure Sale?

The foreclosure sale will be conducted by a trustee (usually from a title insurance company, but a private individual can also conduct the sale). The trustee will cry the sale for the benefit of those in attendance. The trustee's cry (a description of the property to be sold) will be followed by a qualifying check of the bidders in attendance to verify that each has the ability to pay at least the opening bid.

The usual form of acceptable payment is cash or a cashier's check drawn on a California bank. The investor can find out in advance the trustee's requirements by contacting the trustee the day prior to the sale. Sometimes you can negotiate with the trustee to come up with a percentage of the winning bid (see our discussion of IRS auctions in Chapter 12) at the foreclosure sale with the balance to be paid in 30 days.

When You Bid

Bring the amount you are willing to pay for the property and no more. Have the cashier's checks in various denominations so that you can provide the exact amount of your successful bid. Without the checks in various denominations, a refund of your excess money could take several weeks to receive.

It is of utmost importance that you do not share with anyone, or let anyone discover, how much money you have to bid on a property. This will weaken your chances for successful bidding because your competition can form a strategy to squeeze you out.

That is why we recommend you attend several foreclosure auctions to observe what goes on. It is not just important for you to watch the person conducting the foreclosure. It is also important for you to see how your competition operates.

Bidding Rings

You may discover that there is a bidding ring at your foreclosure sales. Although this may be illegal and unethical, you still must be prepared to encounter one. So much the better for you if a bidding ring does not exist.

A bidding ring conspires on who is going to get the winning bid. It works something like this. Three investors get together and agree on who is going to get what property. Investor 1 will get property A. Investor 2 will get property B. Investor 3 will get property C.

When property A comes up for bid, investor 2 and investor 3 will not bid against investor 1. However, if investor 1 is encountering competition from you or other investors, investor 2 and investor 3 may start bidding. They do this for one of two reasons.

The first reason is to try to force you out of the bidding. They do this by trying to make you think there is too much competition for the property, hoping you will back off and wait for another property.

Now, one of the three conspirators will have the bid just higher than yours that is the winning bid. If this is investor 2 or investor 3, they will defer to investor 1 and let investor 1 have the property.

The second reason is to try to bid up the price of the property and stick you with the winning bid. They try to get you so caught up in the frenzy and excitement of the bidding process that you lose your cool. When you lose your cool, you get auction fever. The bidding ring is trying to give you a lethal case of auction fever. We will talk about auction fever shortly.

The point is that once you have overbid on that first property, you may have taken yourself out of the game. Now you don't have the cash to bid on other properties coming up for sale. One and done. You are out of the bidding for the foreclosure sales for that month. That is exactly what the members of the bidding ring want to happen.

Even though you may be anxious to obtain the property, you must keep a poker face. Don't bid too early in the bidding. You will only drive up the price. We have found that in those circumstances where we waited until the hammer went down a second time before we made our first bid, we experienced success.

Auction Fever

Auction fever occurs when you bring more than one buyer into a buying situation. In the normal real estate-buying scenario only one buyer at a time is making an offer on a property. If there are multiple offers, the buyers are not together in the same place, so each buyer's offer is unknown to the other buyers.

At a foreclosure auction all the buyers are compressed in one place at the same time. The bidding is out in the open. Every offer is instantly known to the other buyers. This can create a bidding frenzy. We have seen people at foreclosure auctions actually faint! They became so excited during the bidding process that they passed out.

Bidding can be like an intoxicant. To coin a phrase, "You have to bid in moderation." If you notice you are coming down with auction fever, take deep breaths and stop bidding. We recommend you always take a friend or relative with you to protect against auction fever.

Buying at the Foreclosure Sale

Let's review something we first discussed in Chapter 3. Foreclosure sales are conducted at a public auction. The highest bidder gets the property. The seller at the foreclosure sale is a trustee or representative of the lender. So the sellers at the foreclosure sale are really auctioneers. They are professional sellers. Yet, they do not have any financial stake in the property. They are just doing their job.

Once it gets to the foreclosure sale, the owners are out of luck. If you have not been able to help them, or work out a purchase for their equity, the owners will lose all of their equity at the foreclosure sale.

It is true that the owners can bid at the foreclosure sale. But how will that be possible since you need to have cash to bid? If owners had the cash to bid, they would not be in foreclosure!

Credit Bid The opening bid is called a credit bid. The credit bid is put forward by the trustee, sheriff, or the representative of the lender. The credit bid is the total of the remaining loan balance, payments in default, and any costs associated with the foreclosure sale.

If no one bids above the credit bid, then the lender winds up owning the property. Any bid made above the credit bid has to be made in cash. Let's say the loan amount is $160,000 and the default amount is

$10,000. Let's say the foreclosure sale expenses are $1,900. What would the opening credit bid be?

Opening Credit Bid

Loan Amount	$160,000
Default Amount	$ 10,000
Foreclosure Expenses	$ 1,900
Credit Bid	$171,900

Winning the Bid What if you bid one dollar more than the opening credit bid? When the hammer strikes the third time, and you are the highest bidder, *you own the property!* It is not a conditional contract but one that you must immediately honor.

If you could buy the property at the foreclosure sale for $171,901 would that be a better deal than if you could have bought the property from the owner before the foreclosure sale for $179,000?

The answer is that it depends. While it certainly looks like getting the property at the foreclosure sale for $7,099 less is the better deal, maybe it isn't the better deal. This is a price-versus-terms conversation.

You may get a better price at the foreclosure sale. But you have to come up with almost $172,000! Buying from the owner you didn't get as good a price—$179,000. But you only have $19,000 in the deal. Will that $7,000 lower price be worth tying up an additional $153,000?

In the next chapter we will show you how to flip your foreclosure deals for Quick Cash. This may get you a Quick Cash profit and save you tens of thousands of dollars from out of your pocket to buy the same property at a foreclosure sale. Some of you will get very excited about assigning your foreclosure deals. Some of you will wind up optioning your foreclosure deals. No matter which of these you choose, you can be successful making Quick Cash in foreclosures.

CHAPTER 14

Flipping Foreclosures

Flipping is a two-step process. The first step is to tie up a property. This is otherwise known as making an offer. The second step is to find a buyer. This is known as making money on your deal. This is the point of flipping and is the Quick Cash strategy in action.

When you flip foreclosures, you use the same techniques as flipping non-foreclosures but with a few modifications. In this chapter we will talk about the flipping techniques for all properties and give you the particulars for flipping foreclosures. In fact, the next three chapters all focus on flipping foreclosures. This is where you make Quick Cash in foreclosures.

We will introduce you to our real estate investment axiom: *Buy the property first, then get the financing.* The foreclosure corollary to this axiom is *buy the foreclosure first, then get a buyer.* When you follow these axioms, it makes it easier to write offers. As we have said, writing an offer is the way to tie up a property. When you tie up a property, you control a property.

Tying Up a Property

In the 1990s, when we traveled the country teaching real estate investors Robert Allen's Nothing Down seminars, we blew them away with *buy the property first, then get the financing.* In city after city people told us we could not buy real estate this way.

We told them to try it our way and report back to us what happened. Lo and behold, from Seattle to Orlando, from Los Angeles to Baltimore, from Chicago to Dallas, our students found that they could indeed buy the property first, then get the financing.

Mind-Set

Most, if not all, retail buyers (home buyers) have this mind-set: How much money do I have to put down, and how much of a monthly payment can I afford? With this mind-set, they go to a lender to get prequalified for a real estate loan.

What the real estate lender says determines how much of a house the home buyer thinks he or she can afford. Of course, being prequalified means nothing once you actually apply for a loan. You can be prequalified for a $200,000 loan and actually wind up receiving only a $175,000 loan at closing.

You are a real estate investor and not a home buyer. You are a wholesale buyer of real estate. You are going to do things differently. Everyone, except us, will tell you to get your financing first, then buy the property.

Buy the Foreclosure First, Then Get a Buyer

Example 1

Buy the Foreclosure First We found a four-bedroom, two-bathroom, single-family home. The property was headed to foreclosure. The retail value of the property was $159.000. The seller had an assumable VA loan with a remaining balance of $129,000. The seller was $3,000 behind in his payments. The seller's equity position was $27,000.

Seller's Equity Position

Retail Value	$159,000
First Mortgage	$129,000
Back Payments	$ 3,000
Seller's Equity	$ 27,000

When the agent asked us what we were prequalified for, this was our response (and will be yours). We told the agent that we were real estate investors. If the property met our parameters, we had the financial resources, along with our money partners, to buy the property.

We set up an appointment with the agent and the seller. We made the foreclosure options presentation. At the end of our presentation, the seller said he would like to sell us his property. We offered the seller no money down and agreed to take over payments on the loan and make up the $3,000 in back payments. The seller accepted our offer. The seller would pay his agent the real estate commission.

We did not have to qualify for a new loan. We did not have to qualify to take over the seller's VA loan. We did not have to come up with a down payment. We made an offer that worked for us. We let the seller decide whether to accept our offer. We and you may not have accepted our offer. Why the seller accepted our offer was the seller's business.

Then Get a Buyer We now had a property available to flip. Only by making an offer can you start the process of flipping a property. We flipped the property for $139,000 within two weeks to a retail buyer who was going to live in the property. Why did we flip the property for so cheap a price? Our strategy is Quick Cash. Could we have waited and perhaps gotten a higher price? Yes, but our Quick Cash strategy embraces the principle "A bird in the hand is worth two in the bush."

The buyer was going to assume the VA loan on the property. The buyer was actually a veteran. He was going to use his VA eligibility to assume the loan. The buyer was very happy to get a good deal. The seller was happy because he was out from under the foreclosure with no deficiency judgment hanging over his head. We were happy because we had made $7,000.

Our Profit

Sales Price	$139,000
Purchase Price	$129,000
Back Payments	$ 3,000
Profit	$ 7,000

Example 2

Buy the Foreclosure First We found a three-bedroom, two-bathroom, single-family home with a pool. The property was in foreclosure. The lender had sent the first formal notice of default letter. The sellers were in a panic.

The retail value of the property was $210,000. The first mortgage on the property had a remaining balance of $155,000. The sellers were $9,000 behind in their payments. The sellers' equity position was $46,000.

Seller's Equity Position

Retail Value	$210,000
First Mortgage	$155,000
Back Payments	$ 9,000
Seller's Equity	$ 46,000

We offered the sellers $10,000 for their equity in the form of a promissory note secured by a second trust deed on the property. The promissory note was a straight note for three years. This means there were no payments until the final balloon payment of principal and interest at the end of the three years.

We also agreed to pay the $9,000 in back payments and reinstate the loan. The total cash out of our pocket was $9,000. Remember, the $10,000 we offered the sellers for their equity was a promissory note and not cash. We were not worried about this promissory note because we were going to flip the property.

Then Get a Buyer We flipped the property for $185,000. The buyer was a real estate investor who was planning on renting the property. The buyer assumed the first mortgage of $155,000 from the lender and our second mortgage of $10,000 to the sellers.

We were now off the hook to pay the sellers. Because the $10,000 second mortgage had no payments, the real estate investor would be able to have a positive cash flow.

How did we make out on this deal? We invested $9,000 cash and received our money back plus an $11,000 profit. The sellers avoided foreclosure and had $10,000 plus interest coming their way three years down the road. The investor was happy because she got a good deal.

Our Profit

Retail Value	$185,000
First Mortgage	$155,000
Second Mortgage	$ 10,000
Back Payments	$ 9,000
Profit	$ 11,000

Some of you are thinking, "Why didn't you guys hold on to the property like the investor you flipped the property to, rent it out, and have a positive cash flow?" That is good thinking if you are using the long-term wealth-building strategy. We have a Quick Cash strategy, so landlording is not on our agenda.

Example 3

Buy the Foreclosure First Early on in our real estate investing career, we tied up a three-bedroom, three-bathroom, single-family home with a pool. The seller was in pre-foreclosure. We negotiated a deal with the seller and bought their equity. We then spent $8,000 fixing up the property.

We are presenting this example to coach you on what not to do. This was not one of our finest hours. We were still in the more traditional mind-set of trying to make everyone in the deal happy. By the time this deal blew up, no one was happy.

Then Get a Buyer We found retail buyers who said they were in love with the house. To make the deal work, we agreed to repaint (again!) the inside of the house, which we had just repainted, the colors the buyers wanted.

We also agreed to run a natural gas line to the utility room so the buyers could use their gas dryer. Finally, we had a tree removed from the pool area because the buyers were concerned that the roots were going to crack the bottom of the pool.

Can you guess what happened? The buyers came down with a disease all retail buyers get during the course of a real estate transaction. Some buyers get a mild case of the disease. Some buyers get a severe case of the disease. Unfortunately for us, these particular buyers came down with a terminal case of the disease.

Buyer's Remorse What is this dreaded disease? Buyer's remorse! All buyers experience the onset of the disease, once their offer is accepted by the seller. Even as a real estate investor, you will experience buyer's remorse. There is no known antidote or medication. The disease just has to run its course.

The symptoms of buyer's remorse usually strike at night, when a buyer is about to go to sleep. Sometimes the symptoms strike after the buyer has fallen asleep and they awaken as if from a nightmare.

The buyers start having doubts about the purchase. Are they doing the right thing? Should they look at more properties? Did they offer too much? Can they really afford the monthly payments? Is the house big enough? Is the house too big?

They start to sweat. They get out of bed and get a drink of water. They go back to bed, but they can't fall asleep. The questions begin swirling again in their heads. What if they don't qualify for a loan? What if they *do* qualify for a loan? Who is going to take care of the pool? What if the pool does leak?

In our case, three weeks after we had accepted the buyers' offer, and three days after we had finished repainting, installing the gas line, and removing the tree, the buyers backed out. Their case of remorse became terminal for them and for us. Our deal was dead.

Bottom line: Provide allowances for the work to be done *after* closing, if you must, to make the deal work, but don't spend your time or money on it before closing. Oh yes, and our profit on this deal? Don't ask. You got the point, right?

Example 4

Buy the Foreclosure First The other problem with retail buyers is they usually do not pay cash for their real estate purchases. They have to qualify for and obtain a loan from a real estate lender. This means you will have to wait longer to get your money. Forty-five days is a fairly standard closing period from the time an offer is accepted to get a loan processed and funded.

In the case of a government-insured loan or a government-guaranteed loan such as FHA loans or VA loans, it may take anywhere from 45 to 75 days to fund the loan and close the escrow!

Then Get a Buyer Again, early on in our real estate investing career, we tied up a three-bedroom, one-and-a-half-bathroom condo that was in pre-foreclosure. We bought it for nothing down and took over the seller's existing loan. We flipped the condo to a retail buyer who made an FHA offer to us for $89,000. This looked like a sure moneymaker for us because we only had $2,000 into the property for back payments on the loan.

Our Profit

Sales Price	$89,000
Purchase Price	$77,000
Back Payments	$ 2,000
Profit	$10,000

The escrow was to close in 45 days or sooner. When it finally closed after 79 days, we had several unexpected surprises. The first surprise was that the deal actually closed. That was a nice surprise. The other surprises were not so nice.

We had almost three months of interest due on the old loan being paid off. We had almost three months of property taxes to pay. And we had almost three months of homeowner association dues to pay as well. These costs were really starting to add up.

The coup de grâce was the four discount points we had to pay for the buyer on the $84,000 FHA government-insured loan. Each discount point was 1 percent of the loan amount. This amounted to $840! We had no idea this was going to be so expensive. Needless to say, we were not happy with what happened to our $10,000 potential profit.

Actual Profit

Potential Profit	$10,000
Loan Interest	$ 1,540
Property Taxes	$ 750
Homeowner's Dues	$ 353
FHA Discount Points	$ 3,360
Actual Profit	$ 3,997

Wholesale Buyers

We actually prefer flipping our foreclosure properties to wholesale buyers. Wholesale buyers do not get buyer's remorse. (Well maybe a little bit.) We know some of you are thinking: "Wait a minute. How can you make any money flipping real estate to wholesale buyers? Don't wholesale buyers want to pay a wholesale price?"

We do flip our foreclosure investments at a wholesale price to wholesale buyers! We are not greedy about it. We prefer to do many smaller deals and make a quick profit rather than one or two big deals that are very time-consuming and that entail more risk.

We have come to appreciate that being successful real estate investors is strictly a numbers game. Although we prefer to flip our foreclosures to other investors for all the reasons we just talked about, we are still smart people. Our marketplace is both retail and wholesale buyers. The more buyers you have in your potential pool, the more likely you will be able to flip your foreclosures successfully.

In the next chapter we will show you how to assign your foreclosure contracts. This speeds up the flipping time. Rather than you taking title to the property, you may never have to take title to the foreclosure property to make Quick Cash. The buyer you assign your contract to will receive title directly from the owner. Fasten your seat belts!

CHAPTER 15

Assigning Foreclosures

Our number-one way we flip foreclosures is through assigning real estate contracts. This is a way to flip real estate without buying or owning the property. You may not even have to close escrow. We really are not flipping real estate at all. To flip real estate, technically, you need to *own* the real estate.

We are flipping real estate *contracts.* Real estate contracts are personal property. We own the contracts. Once you know how to assign contracts, your real estate investing career is going to take off.

We will give you the information you need to understand assigning contracts. We will talk about the types of contracts you can assign. We will then apply assigning to the foreclosure arena and show you how to make Quick Cash assigning your foreclosure contracts.

What Is Assigning?

Assigning a real estate contract transfers your position in the contract to another person for a fee. Said technically, assigning a real estate contract allows you, the assignor, to assign the contract to a new person, the assignee. An assignment transfers your rights to purchase a property under the terms of a real estate purchase contract to a new buyer.

The new buyer literally steps into your shoes and can buy the property under the same terms and conditions you negotiated with the seller. The assignor gives paperwork—the assignment—to the assignee, who receives the paperwork in return for money or other valuable consideration.

Assignment Fees

The money you receive for assigning a contract is called an assignment fee. The fee is negotiable between you, the assignor, and the person you assign the contract to, the assignee. The other party to the contract you have had accepted—seller, lessor, optionor, lender, or whomever—has no say in your negotiations with your assignee.

What should the fee be that you receive for assigning a contract? We have assigned a contract for as little as $1,000. We have also assigned a contract for as much as $100,000. Typically, the fees we have received for assigning contracts range between $5,000 and $15,000.

Types of Real Estate Contracts That You Can Assign

Virtually every type of real estate contract can be assigned. You can assign purchase contracts, options, leases, lease options, mortgage contracts, trust deeds, . . . the list goes on. You can even assign an assignment contract! If it is a real estate contract, you can figure out a way to assign it. Assigning a contract is the easiest and quickest way to flip real estate.

Purchase Contracts

The complete name for a purchase contract is actually "purchase contract for real estate and deposit receipt." This is the contract that contains the terms and conditions to which you and the seller agree when the seller accepts your offer to purchase their property.

We have included a blank purchase contract along with other useful contract forms in Appendix C. You can access the Texas Real Estate Commission's contract at www.trec.state.tx.us/. Office supply stores in your area may carry a generic real estate purchase contract. Or you can use a purchase contract from a local real estate company.

The truth of the matter is that you can use a napkin at a restaurant to write a real estate offer. We don't recommend using napkins to write your offers, however—the ink runs on the napkin when it gets wet. (We've had it happen.) As long as the purchase contract is in writing, it is valid. Every state has a statute of frauds, which says that for a real estate contract to be valid, it must be in writing.

If you are working with a real estate agent and they want to use their contract, then use their contract. It is not worth the aggravation spending the time to educate a real estate agent on why you should use your contract. Just make sure everything you want in the contract is communicated by whatever purchase contract you use.

You'll want to include everything you can possibly think of in your purchase contract. Every blank space is either filled in, or the letters NA (not applicable) are written in. You are negotiating not just for yourself but also for the buyer to whom you are going to assign the contract.

Believe us when we tell you the new buyer wants a really good deal! How the new buyer gets a really good deal is when you write a really good contract that you have accepted from the property owner.

Your state may require special wording if you are purchasing a homeowner's equity in pre-foreclosure. We have already mentioned the wording required by the State of California in the pre-foreclosure phase. Remember, the pre-foreclosure phase lasts until the foreclosure sale occurs, no matter what the state of the property is.

Deposit Receipt There is a deposit receipt section in every real estate purchase contract. Sometimes this is referred to as the earnest money deposit. This is where the buyer includes some type of valuable consideration with the contract to show good faith to the seller. In other words, the deposit the buyer attaches to the offer shows that he or she is earnest about buying the property.

We recommend using a promissory note as your deposit instrument for all your contracts for two reasons. First, by using a promissory note, you protect your cash. Second, you don't want 10, 15, or 20 personal checks out there accompanying all those offers you are writing and presenting.

You only have to turn the promissory note into cash if your offer is accepted and you are going to open an escrow. If you assign your purchase contract before you open escrow, then the promissory note never gets cashed.

The promissory note we recommend you use can be found in Appendix C. It is in the format of a check. You may be able to find a similar promissory note in the legal forms section of an office supply store.

This is a much simpler version than the promissory note used by lenders as evidence of the debt for a real estate loan. The main idea here is to have something attached to the purchase contract that represents consideration. This gives validity to your contract.

Option Contracts

A real estate option contract says you will buy a property within a certain time frame. You will commit funds in the form of an option fee or option money to keep the option open for the agreed-upon period of time.

Option contracts have a unique feature among all the different real estate contracts. All contracts are originally bilateral. Consent in the form of mutual agreement on both the seller's part and the buyer's part is necessary for validity. Once the option has been agreed to, only the buyer can exercise it.

The seller can't back out of the deal if the buyer exercises the option. The optionee (buyer) can back out of the deal and not be sued for specific performance. The optionor (seller) gets to keep the option fee the optionee put up, but that's all.

We use an option contract that is designed to be assigned by the wording of the contract itself. See our book *The New Path to Real Estate Wealth: Earning Without Owning* for a copy of this option contract. In the event you are using an option contract that is not set up to be assigned, all you have to do is add the words "and/or assigns" to the buyer's name portion of the contract.

Leases, Lease Options, Mortgage Contracts, and Trust Deeds

Every type of real estate contract can be assigned. Leases, lease options, mortgage contracts, and trust deeds can be assigned. Even an assignment contract can be assigned.

Car dealers use assignments in their rebate programs. Assigning contracts is everywhere in the business world. The point is that we want you to feel comfortable assigning real estate contracts.

How to Assign a Contract

Assigning a contract begins when you write the initial offer. In the initial offer you make to the owner, whether it is a purchase contract, an option contract, a mortgage contract, or a trust deed, you use the terminology *and/or assigns* in the contract.

You have a new name from this day forth. Think of it as if you are being given a royal title. This title is much better than *sir or madam.* It is even better than *your royal highness.* It is more powerful than *your majesty.* From now on, as a real estate investor writing contracts, you will be known as: *Your Name and/or assigns.*

Assignment Contract

We have shown you how to assign a real estate contract using the *and/or assigns* name addition. What about an actual assignment contract? We find that having an assignment contract available makes assigning any contract a more viable option.

You still want *and/or assigns* in the buyer's name section in whatever contract you are writing. By using the assignment contract in conjunction with *and/or assigns,* you build an added layer of written protection for yourself, the owner of the property, and the new buyer.

Assigning a contract is completely aboveboard and legal. When an owner asks you what *and/or assigns* means, this is what you should say.

And/Or Assigns Script "________________ (Owner's Name), the and/or assigns clause gives both you and us the added flexibility of bringing in additional buyers or money partners to successfully close our transaction. Would that be all right with you?"

In our experience, the owner's answer has always been yes. Sometimes we have had to work with owners a while and educate them on the benefits that this phrase has for them. All you are trying to do with *and/or assigns* is create flexibility.

What do you do if the owner's answer is no? You want to make sure the owner understands what you are trying to do by having the ability to assign your contract. Flexibility is the name of the game in making a real estate deal work.

Flexibility on your part and the owner's part is especially important in a pre-foreclosure real estate deal. If the owner will not agree to give you the flexibility you need by having *and/or assigns* in your contract, let the owner know that you will not proceed to present the rest of the contract.

You must stick to your guns on this point. *And/or assigns* is that important to your real estate investing success. It is much harder to come back to the negotiating table after you have already reached an agreement with the owner. Have *and/or assigns* part of your agreement from the beginning. See our book *The New Path to Real Estate Wealth: Earning Without Owning* for a copy of our assignment contract.

Why Use an Assignment?

There are four main reasons for using an assignment. Assigning a purchase contract makes you money without buying the property. Assigning is the fastest way to flip a property. Assigning is the quickest way to make money in real estate investing. Assigning avoids all the pitfalls of real estate ownership.

Assigning Makes You Money without Buying Property

Assigning a real estate contract makes you money without buying property. In a traditional real estate investment, you (the investor) make money by finding a property, writing and having your offer accepted by the seller, opening and successfully closing an escrow, fixing up the property (if necessary), and then selling the property to a buyer. This is what a timeline would look like for buying real estate to make money:

Buying Timeline for Buying Real Estate to Make Money

Find property	Write offer	Offer accepted	Open escrow	Close escrow	Fix up	Sell property
				Spend money	Spend money	Make money

We are being rather generous with the timeline. It is actually harder than that. The reality of making money when you buy real estate the traditional way begins with that timeline. You really don't make any money until you do the following: advertise and show the property, receive and accept an offer, and open and close an escrow. Then, and only then, do you make money.

Selling Timeline for Buying Real Estate to Make Money

Advertise property	Show property	Receive offer	Accept offer	Open escrow	Close escrow
Spend money					Make money

Assigning Is the Fastest Way to Flip Property

Assigning a real estate contract is the fastest way to flip property. Let's face it. Paperwork is the name of the game in real estate investing. The less paperwork involved in a real estate transaction, the better.

The less paperwork involved in a real estate transaction means the less time it takes to complete the transaction. The less time involved on your part and the real estate investor or retail buyer you are assigning the contract to means a faster turnaround time for you.

Paperwork for Flipping without Escrow This is the paperwork involved in the simplest flip we do. This is a no-money-down deal. There is no escrow involved. We write a purchase contract and promissory note, which we present to the property owner. The owner accepts our offer. The owner gives us back our promissory note and a quitclaim deed to transfer title to the property. This makes three distinct pieces of paperwork for the buying side.

Flip Paperwork for Buying Property

1. Real Estate Purchase Contract

2. Promissory Note

3. Quitclaim Deed

We receive a purchase contract and a personal check as an earnest money deposit from an investor we flip the property to. We give the real estate investor a quitclaim deed.

The investor gives us a cashier's check. We give the investor back his or her personal check. Again, we don't have an escrow between the investor and us. We have an additional four distinct pieces of paperwork on the selling side.

Flip Paperwork for Selling Side

1. Real Estate Purchase Contract

2. Personal Check

3. Quitclaim Deed

4. Cashier's Check

Now we have a total of seven distinct pieces of paperwork involved in this transaction: three pieces of paperwork on the buying side and four pieces of paperwork on the selling side.

Paperwork for Assignment What if we just assigned our purchase contract instead of doing a traditional flip where we actually owned something? Would we speed up the flip by doing an assignment? How much paperwork is involved if we assign our purchase contract?

We write a purchase contract and a promissory note, which we present to the owner. The owner gives us back our promissory note. So far everything is the same as doing a flip.

Here is where the assignment transaction changes the paperwork. The owner does not give us a quitclaim deed. The owner gives a quitclaim deed to transfer title to the investor to whom we assign the purchase contract. We now have one less quitclaim deed using the assignment.

The next paperwork that changes with the assignment is that there is no second purchase contract. We do not receive a purchase contract from the investor. The investor takes over our position in the first purchase contract.

The investor does not write a personal check to accompany his or her offer to us. We receive a cashier's check from the investor. The investor receives the quitclaim deed from the owner.

Assignment Paperwork

1. Real Estate Purchase Contract

2. Promissory Note

3. Quitclaim Deed

4. Cashier's Check

The difference in the amount of paperwork for a flip and an assignment is substantial. The flip paperwork includes seven items. The assignment paperwork includes four items.

Our point is that assigning a contract is the fastest way to flip property. Assigning a contract is flipping property! Flipping is good. When you use assigning as a flipping tactic, you'll streamline the paperwork and reduce the time involved in the transaction. You'll also make the same amount of money on the deal.

Assigning Is the Quickest Way to Make Money

Assigning a real estate contract is the fastest way to make money in real estate investing. When you have a Quick Cash strategy, time is definitely of the essence.

The timeline for assigning contracts is substantially shorter than the timeline for a traditional real estate investment. Even with flipping a property, you can't make money as quickly as when you assign contracts.

As you can see, you can make money quicker and at more junctures along the way than with a traditional real estate investment strategy of buy the property, own the property, and sell the property.

Assigning Timeline

Find property	Write offer	Offer accepted	Open escrow	Close escrow	Fix up	Sell property
	Make money	Make money	Make money	Make money		

Assigning Avoids the Pitfalls of Real Estate Ownership

Assigning a contract avoids all the pitfalls of real estate ownership. We feel that assigning is the best strategy for the foreclosure arena. Assigning foreclosure has multiple advantages to the traditional foreclosure investment strategy.

These advantages include no landlording, no monthly mortgage payments, no property taxes, no hazard insurance, no maintenance costs, no homeowner association dues, no lawsuits, no extensive record keeping, and no income tax problems.

When to Assign a Contract

You can assign a real estate contact before, during, and after the closing. Assigning a contract before the closing is the way we like to do our own transactions. You tie up a property with an accepted contract and immediately search for a buyer to whom to assign the contract.

Assigning a contract during the closing is our second-favorite way we like to do our transactions. You tie up the property and assign the contract before the closing takes place. The assignee takes your place in the closing and then winds up closing the escrow.

Assigning after the closing is the final way we like to do our transactions. Again, you tie up a property with an assignment clause in the contract. If you don't find a buyer before closing and wind up closing the property yourself, you can quickly transfer your interest in the property to another buyer after closing. Essentially, you are going to flip the property using what we call an assignment deed.

Look at the timeline for assigning contracts. This will give you a way to visualize the different times you can use an assignment. Anytime you can assign a contract and make money is a good time to do an assignment.

The timeline is the same for assigning in the foreclosure arena. You can assign your contract after you write the offer to buy the owner's equity and before an escrow is opened. You can assign your contract to buy the owner's equity during the escrow. You can also assign your contract to buy the owner's equity after closing escrow.

Timeline for Assigning Contracts

Write offer **Open escrow** **Close escrow**

Assign before closing **Assign during closing** **Assign after closing**

Assignment before Closing

We don't ever want to close an escrow. At least not in the traditional way most real estate investors do. We want to "close" our deals in a different way. In the normal course of events a real estate transaction goes like this.

A real estate investor finds a potential property. The investor writes an offer on the property and presents it to the owner. There is a negotiation back and forth between the owner and the investor. There is an agreement as to price and terms. Then the owner and the investor open an escrow or go to a closing.

Once the escrow is complete, the escrow closes. The owner receives money or other valuable consideration from the investor. The investor receives the title to and possession of the property.

Close by Assigning We close our deals by assigning our owner-accepted real estate contracts. By using an assignment of contract, we use a one-page escrow instruction between us and the buyer to whom we are assigning the contract. In the case of a foreclosure we have the owner give a quitclaim deed to the new buyer.

Assignment during Closing

An assignment during closing is a very common occurrence in our real estate investing. We have said that our favorite time period to do an assignment is before closing, but doing an assignment during closing runs a close second.

The difference between assigning before closing or during closing is whether you have formally opened escrow. An assignment before closing means you have written an offer and had it accepted but have not opened escrow before you assign the contract. An assignment during closing means you have done all of the above and opened an escrow.

The new buyer steps into your position as the buyer in the escrow. The assignment fee can come to you through the escrow or outside the escrow. Either way is fine.

An escrow will be opened for two reasons. If the owner requests an escrow, an escrow will be opened. If the new buyer requests an escrow with the owner, an escrow will be opened.

Assignment after Closing

At first blush it might seem out of place for us to talk about assigning after the closing. However, as we have taught you to do with every contract you write, you used the clause *and/or assigns* when you wrote the purchase contract.

What do you do if you decide to close the transaction yourself because it is such a good deal or you have not found a new buyer before the closing date comes?

The fastest way to assign your interest in a property after you have closed escrow is to quitclaim the property to a new buyer. Whatever interest or title you have in the property is transferred to the buyer.

We are the only people who will tell you that you can assign a piece of real estate after you have closed escrow. We call a quitclaim deed an assignment deed. We use this deed when we want to quickly get out of a property that we wind up owning.

Once you assimilate the assigning tactic into your foreclosure investing strategy, you will begin to find all kinds of contracts to assign. Real estate contracts to assign will begin to find you. We look to assign every foreclosure contract we write.

In the next chapter we will show you how to use real estate option contracts to make Quick Cash in foreclosures. There are many advantages to using an option contract in general. When you see the advantages of using an option contract in the foreclosure arena, you are going to get very excited. Of course, we will recommend you think about assigning your real estate option contract!

CHAPTER 16

Optioning Foreclosures

A real estate option contract gives you the right to buy a property without the obligation of having to buy it. In a normal purchase contract, when the buyer and seller have a meeting of the minds and sign the contract, the buyer must perform and go through with the agreed-upon purchase. If the buyer does not perform based on the terms of the contract, the seller can sue the buyer for specific performance.

An option contract allows the buyer and seller to have a meeting of the minds, sign the option contract, and offer the buyer a time certain to exercise the option. If the buyer does not exercise the option, the option expires, and the buyer owes no further obligation to the seller.

Put another way, an option contract gives a potential buyer the right to purchase a property before the specified future date in the contract for the amount and under the terms and conditions written in the contract.

Optionor/Optionee

In an option contract the parties to the contract are the optionor and the optionee. The optionor gives real estate paperwork—the option contract—to the optionee. In return the optionee gives money to the optionor for granting the option. This is called the option fee. The seller is the optionor. The buyer is the optionee.

Option Fee

The option fee is the consideration given by the optionee to the optionor. This is what satisfies the consideration requirement and makes an option contract valid. As we have said, in return for the option fee, the optionor gives the option to the optionee to purchase the property.

The option fee is usually a percentage of the agreed-upon purchase price for the property. This percentage can range from as low as 0.5 percent on a higher-priced property to as much as 10 percent on a lower-priced property. For a $100 million purchase price the option fee may be $500,000. On a $300,000 purchase price the option fee may be $30,000.

Option Fee Percentages

$100,000,000	Purchase Price	$300,000
× 0.5%	Option Percent	× 10%
$ 500,000	Option Fee	$ 30,000

The option fee can be applied to the purchase price in the event that the optionee exercises the option to purchase. Sometimes the option fee does not apply to the purchase price. This may happen when a second or third option time period is negotiated. We always negotiate the option fee applying to the purchase price. That way, if we exercise the option, we already have past money credited to the deal.

Option Fee Applied to Purchase Price We made an offer on a five-bedroom, four-bathroom, 5,000-square-foot, single-family home in a great neighborhood. Our offer was in the form of an option contract. We wanted a six-month option period because we were concerned about which way the real estate market was headed.

Were we still in the prosperity phase of the real estate cycle? Or were we headed into a recession? If the real estate market was still going in an upward direction, we would buy the property. If the real estate market was headed in a downward direction, we were not going to buy the property.

We negotiated the option fee to be applied toward the purchase price if we exercised the option. If we did not exercise the option, the seller would keep the option fee. In this case the option fee was $2,500. Although this was a very small percentage of the $300,000 purchase price, the seller still accepted our contract.

Option Fee

Purchase Price	$300,000
Option Fee	$ 2,500
Remaining Balance	$297,500

Option Fee Not Applied to Purchase More frequently than you might expect, the negotiated option fee does not apply to the purchase price. Home builders often acquire finished lots for construction through option contracts with a real estate developer.

In many cases the home builder will want to extend the option past the original time period. Let's say the first option period was for six months. An extension could be needed by the home builder because the builder was unprepared to start building.

To extend the option period for another six months, the developer may require another option fee from the builder. Sometimes the second option period may be extended to a third or even a fourth option. Although the developer may have been willing to apply the first option fee toward the purchase price of the lots, the developer may not be willing to apply any of the other fees to the purchase price once an extension or extensions are agreed to.

Why Use an Option?

When you use a real estate option contract, you can tie up a property without revealing your interest in the property. It gives you the right to buy the property without revealing your identity. Once you close on a property, your name is revealed in the public record as the buyer of the property. You can wait to exercise your option until you have put together all the pieces to your overall real estate plan.

Walt Disney assembled the property for Walt Disney World in Florida using option contracts. He did not want to tip his hand to the many different property owners from whom he needed to purchase property. If remaining property owners knew he was buying property, they could hold out for a higher price. Disney would have had to pay big bucks once word got out that he wanted to put all the properties together for Walt Disney World.

Ten Reasons to Use an Option Contract

1. Maintain Privacy If it was good enough for Walt Disney, it's good enough for us. As we have said, when you close escrow on a property, the grant deed or warranty deed is recorded. This deed becomes part of the public record. This means anyone in the world can get on the Internet and find out who owns that property. Why? Because the deed names the grantor, the seller, and the grantee, the buyer—that's you.

2. Protect Your Cash Just like with the stock market, where you can protect your cash by using a stock option, using a real estate option protects the amount of cash you have in any single investment. Rather than buying property with 100 percent of your cash, by using an option you control 100 percent of the property with only a small percentage of the cash.

3. Limited Risk/High Return Using an option contract limits your risk as an investor and gives you a high return. Leverage has always been one of the benefits of real estate investing. If you think the investment return is good using the leverage available in a standard real estate transaction, how good do you think the investment return is using an option?

What would the return on our investment be if we used a $20,000 option to tie up a $200,000 property for one year? Let's assume a 5 percent appreciation on the value of the property.

Leverage

Option Fee (10%)	$ 20,000
Purchase Price	$200,000

Appreciation

Purchase Price	$200,000
Annual Appreciation	× 5%
Value Increase	$ 10,000

Return on Investment

Value Increase	$10,000
Amount Invested	$20,000
Investment Return	50%

4. Control Property The name of the game in real estate investing is control. Donald Trump controls more real estate than he owns. When you have control of something, you are oftentimes in a better position than when you own something. Our Quick Cash investment strategy is based on controlling property, not owning property. We take this one step further by controlling property with the paperwork of real estate. By using an option contract you can control lots of property without owning any of it.

Briefly, the advantages of controlling property without owning it include Quick Cash, no landlording, no monthly mortgage payments, no property taxes, no hazard insurance, no maintenance costs, no homeowner association dues, no lawsuits, no extensive record keeping, and no income tax problems.

The advantages of controlling property with an option contract are the same as the advantages to flipping property. Except it is better with the option contract because you can flip the contract rather than flipping the property. In other words, with an option contract you control the property without owning it.

Let's add some numbers to this controlling-property-with-options scenario. How much property could you control using $2.4 million as option fees? Some of you can do the numbers in your head. $2.4 million is 10 percent of what number? That's right—$2.4 million is 10 percent of $24 million. No wonder Donald Trump likes to use real estate options.

Leverage

Option Fee (10%)	$ 2,400,000
Purchase Price	$24,000,000

5. Buy Time By using an option contract you can buy time. You may need time to bring in a money partner. You may need time to get your financing together. You may need time to find a new buyer.

Now is a good time to talk about money partners. There is a ton of money out there looking for a good real estate investment. Our experience as investors has been that finding the right property and/or the right seller is much harder than finding a money partner.

If you're the kind of person who has a lot of money to invest in real estate, congratulations! We wish you good luck in finding a good deal. Unless you find someone like us in your area, you will wind up paying too much for your properties. Of course, you could always contact us. We do business anywhere!

As we told you throughout Chapter 14, *buy the property first, then get the financing.* Most people think of a money partner as someone who puts up the down payment or can pay all cash for the property. Sometimes finding a money partner is finding someone who will put up his or her credit or ability to get a real estate loan.

During the time we were writing this book, we found an ad for a property that was advertised $1 million *under market.* We wrote an offer on the property in the form of a real estate option contract. This is a property we are thinking about keeping for ourselves.

We will use the option period to find a money partner who will qualify for and obtain a loan to be used to purchase the property. We plan on assigning the option to purchase the property if we decide we are not going to keep the property.

6. Assemble Partners We use an option contract when we need to assemble partners to go in on a real estate transaction. Sometimes these partners are money partners. Sometimes they are developers. Sometimes they are home builders. Sometimes they are your real estate team for your area.

You may need to find a real estate attorney. You may need an escrow company or closing agent. What about a title insurance company or even a termite company? You may need to find a real estate agent.

Whatever the partnership needs are to put together a successful transaction, by using a real estate option, you will give yourself the necessary time to form the partnership(s).

7. Watch the Direction of the Market You can use an option to tie up a property and watch the direction of the market. Everyone has 20/20 hindsight with regard to the turning points of the real estate market. The trick is to have 20/20 foresight with regard to these turning points. When things are going well, that is easy to recognize. When things are going not so well, that is easy to recognize.

As we already noted, the economic cycle is one of expansion, prosperity, recession, and depression. Then it repeats itself. Real estate value is greatly influenced by the economic cycle. Typically, real estate is said to do well in the expansion and prosperity phases and poorly in the recession and depression phases.

8. Handle Contingencies We use an option contract when we know there are going to be contingencies that need to be handled as part of the purchase contract. A contingency in a contract is a condition that has to be met, satisfied, or accomplished; otherwise, the whole deal can be blown out of the water.

When you are buying the owner's equity in a pre-foreclosure situation, you may have to handle several contingencies. Can you take over the owner's loan? Will you be able to get clear title? Can you find a buyer to whom you can assign the purchase contract?

We recommend you consider using an option contract to purchase the owner's equity. After you have handled all the contingencies, then you exercise your option and purchase the equity.

9. Procure Financing By using an option contract you can take your time procuring the best-available financing for your real estate deal. We have seen interest rates for real estate loans go from historical highs in the early 1980s to historical lows in the early 2000s.

By doing a 6-month, 12-month, 18-month, or even longer option period, you should be able to find an attractive interest rate to finance the transaction. If not, then you do not have to exercise your option.

10. Income Tax Planning When you use an option contract, you can get certain income tax advantages as an investor. You may want to use an option contract if you are involved in an Internal Revenue Code section 1031 tax-deferred exchange.

When doing a 1031 exchange, the process sometimes becomes a chicken-and-egg debate. Which comes first? Do you sell the property you have and then look for a property to buy? Or do you find a property to buy and then sell the property you have?

We recommend you buy the property you want to exchange into using an option contract. When you find a buyer for the property you are exchanging out of, then you exercise your option and buy the property you want to complete the exchange.

How to Option

Optioning begins with the option contract. You can take a standard purchase contract and turn it into an option contract. Or you can use an option contract from the beginning.

A real estate option contract is similar to a grant deed or warranty deed in that only the seller needs to sign the document to make it valid. Just like in a grant deed or warranty deed, the seller will be granting something in an option contract.

In a grant deed or warranty deed the seller is granting title or ownership in the property to the buyer. In an option contract the seller grants the right for the buyer to buy the property during the option period for a price agreed on in the contract.

Purchase Contracts

You can start with a purchase contract and turn it into an option contract. To do this, go to the supplements section. This is the section in the purchase contract that states that the attached documents are incorporated into the purchase contract. Add the real estate option contract to this section. Attach the option contract to the purchase contract.

The two contracts together become one contract when the option is exercised. You can find a copy of the option contract we use in our book *The New Path to Real Estate Wealth: Earning Without Owning.*

Option Contracts

We recommend using an option contract from the beginning of the transaction. That way both you and the seller know you are interested in putting together an option at the outset of negotiations.

Memorandum of Option A memorandum of option can be recorded to protect your optionee interest in the property. Your name as the optionee does not have to appear on the memorandum of option.

If the optionor/seller does try to sell the property to another buyer during your option period, a title company doing a title search for the other buyer will uncover the recorded memorandum of option. This will prevent the seller from transferring clear title, and the deal with the other buyer will fall apart.

Assigning an Option Contract We use an option contract that is already set up to be assigned by the wording in the contract itself. In the event you are using an option contract that is not set up to be assigned, all you have to do is add the words *and/or assigns* to the buyer's name portion of the contract.

Lease Option Contract A lease option contract can be known by several other names. It may be called a lease with purchase option. It may be called a residential lease with option to purchase. No matter what it is called, its purpose is to combine a lease with an option to purchase.

In a standard lease the lessor, the property owner, gives a lease to the lessee, the tenant. In return the lessee pays the lessor rent. In a standard option the optionor, the property owner, gives an option the optionee, a potential buyer. In return the optionee pays the optionor an option fee.

In a lease option the lessor/optionor, the property owner, gives a lease and an option to the lessee/optionee, the tenant. In return the lessee/optionee pays the lessor/optionor rent. There is no option fee in addition to the rent.

The lease may require a deposit to be applied to a security deposit, a key deposit, a cleaning deposit, last month's rent, and/or whatever else the landlord wants. These deposits are not an option fee.

When to Option

As we have already said, by using a real estate option contract you can control property without buying it. In foreclosure investing timing is everything. You need to be in the right place at the right time. You also have to use the right investing tools at the right time.

Lawsuits, Creditors, Divorce, and IRS Liens

Aside from not tipping off surrounding property owners and potential competition, there are four more important situations when it may be in your best interest to use an option contract to protect your privacy. These include being involved in a lawsuit, being hounded by creditors, going through a divorce, and having the IRS on your case.

Lawsuits When you own real estate, you are a target. Attorneys file lawsuits against people they think have assets worth going after.

Attorneys take on clients for a percentage of the money the attorney can win in court.

How many of you have heard the expression "you can't get blood out of a turnip"? When an attorney is searching the public records to find your real estate assets, you want them to think you are a turnip.

Creditors When creditors come after you, what do they come after? They may not be able to get your home, but they certainly can come after your real estate investments. What real estate investments?

Divorce If your ex-spouse is trying to get money out of you, the first place his or her attorney will look is to your real estate investments. Again, what real estate investments?

IRS Liens Don't even get us started on the IRS or your state taxing authority. If you don't pay the taxing authority what they think you owe them, they will put tax liens on your real estate assets. When you go to sell these assets, the tax lien will show up against the title to your property.

So if you are involved in one of these situations, we recommend using options. You can be a real estate investor who controls property without owning it. We are firm believers in the right to privacy in business affairs. Make using options part of your privacy protection.

Options and Foreclosure

We are going to conclude this chapter on optioning foreclosures with examples of using an option contract in the foreclosure arena. You may want to use an option to tie up the owner's equity in pre-foreclosure. You may want to use an option to help an owner get their hands on some cash in return for your having an equity interest in the property. Let's take a look.

Tie Up the Owner's Equity

In Chapter 8 we talked about buying the owner's equity. We are going to bring back that situation and show you how to buy the owner's equity with an option contract. You are really tying up the owner's equity with the option. You won't exercise your option and buy the equity until you have another buyer to flip your option contract to. Remember the foreclosure situation. We will bring back just enough of the elements of your offer to buy the owner's equity in Chapter 8 so we can contrast this with optioning the owner's equity.

Foreclosure Situation

Foreclosure Value	$185,000
Mortgage	$150,000
Owner's E'quity	$ 35,000

Your Offer to Buy the Equity Instead of the owner's equity being $60,000 in the non-foreclosure situation (when the value was $200,000 and the mortgage was $140,000), the owner's equity is $35,000 in the foreclosure situation. The owner has suffered a $25,000 loss in equity.

You are going to offer the owner $10,000 for the $35,000 equity. If you keep the property, you are going to have to pay the lender the $10,000 in back payments to stop the foreclosure. Now you will have $20,000 in the property. If you have to make repairs and do fix up, you may have $3,000 to $5,000 more involved.

Then you add in mortgage payments, property tax payments, and insurance payments. Resale costs could add another $5,000 to $10,000 or more to your investment. When you add this all up, your total is $30,000 to $35,000!

Your Offer

Cash to Owner	$10,000
Cash to Lender	$10,000
Repairs and Fix Up	$ 5,000
Carrying and Resale Costs	$10,000
Total Invested	$35,000

Your Offer to Option the Equity Put the same contract together with the owner to buy the owner's equity. But make it an option to buy his or her equity. Rather than giving the owner $10,000 up front, give the owner a $1,000 option fee, which applies to the $10,000 if you exercise the option.

You now have protected your cash to the tune of $9,000. You have tied up the property. You have bought time to find another investor or buyer to flip your option to. The way we recommend you flip your option is by assigning it to the next buyer.

If you do not find a buyer to assign your option to, you have two choices. You can walk away from the deal and be out your $1,000 option fee. And the owner cannot sue you for specific performance.

Or you can exercise the option yourself and fix the property. Then you can sell the property to a retail buyer. Either way, by using the option, you can make money through maintaining control of the property.

Making Money with an Option

Retail Buyer		***Wholesale Buyer***	
Sales Price:	$200,000	Flip Fee:	$10,000
Mortgage:	$140,000	Mortgage:	0
Gross Profit:	$ 60,000	Gross Profit:	$10,000
Invested Money:	$ 35,000	Invested Money:	0
Net Profit:	$ 25,000	Net Profit:	$10,000

Buy-Back Option

We call this use of an option "having your cake and eating it, too." If your first offer to the owner in pre-foreclosure to buy their equity meets with a rejection, try using the buy-back option technique.

Normally, the buy-back option is used in any situation in which someone must take the risk of sacrificing part of their equity and future appreciation in exchange for getting their hands on some immediate cash. This exactly describes the owner in pre-foreclosure.

Using a buy-back option is similar to doing an equity share with the owners. Instead of the owners giving you an option, you give the owners an option! You present the same offer to buy the owners' equity that they previously rejected.

However, now you add the feature that you will give them a buy-back option if they will accept your offer. Let's put some numbers to this so you can see the beauty of the buy-back option.

Using the previous example, you give the owners the option to buy back the property within six months for $200,000. It will be as if you fixed the property up, held on to it for six months, and sold it to a retail buyer.

Making Money with a Back Option

Sales Price	$200,000
Mortgage	$140,000
Gross Profit	$ 60,000
Invested Money	$ 35,000
Net Profit	$ 25,000

If you decide to flip the property to another investor, the owners will still have the right to exercise the buy-back option. The other investor will then be selling the property for a retail price.

In the next chapter we will show you how to buy foreclosed property from the lender. These are properties that have moved from the lender's loan portfolio to the lender's property portfolio. They are now real estate-owned—REOs.

CHAPTER 17

Buying from the Lender

What about buying from the lender after the foreclosure sale? Usually, the lender has the biggest financial stake in the property. After all, they made an 80, 90, 95, 97, or even 100 percent loan to the borrower to buy the property to begin with. Can you get a better deal from the lender once the property goes out of the lender's loan portfolio and into the lender's property portfolio? We think the answer is yes.

Lenders' property portfolios are called real estate-owned portfolios, or REOs for short. As we have said, with VA REOs, some investors call them repos (short for repossessions). Real estate lenders are in the business of making real estate loans. Real estate lenders are not in the business of owning real estate. While lenders want to sell their REOs for as much as possible, they also want to move these REO properties as quickly as possible.

The REO Department

Our recommendation to you is to work with several lenders' REO departments and see what happens. You may find a niche working with one contact in one lender's REO department. Once you can put together your first deal, you have a track record with that lender.

Your contact person will then start calling you with other deals perhaps before they become open to the public. We say it this way: *Contacts with people create opportunities. Contacts create contracts.*

Price

There are only two major concerns for you as a real estate investor in a real estate deal. The first major concern is the price you can get a property for after all is said and done. What is the rock-bottom price the owner will accept?

What about the price when you are dealing with REOs? We have already said that we think you can get a better deal from the lender after the foreclosure sale if the property doesn't sell. The lender is now the owner of the property. Getting rid of the property is now the lender's number-one priority.

Terms

The second major concern is the terms you can get a property for after all is said and done. Usually, if sellers get their price, the buyers get their terms. If buyers get their price, sellers get their terms.

For example, we will pay full price to a seller if we get our terms. What are our terms? We want to make no down payment. We want the seller to carry 100 percent of the financing. We want to make no monthly payments on the seller financing. If we get our price, we will give the sellers their terms. If the seller accepts our wholesale price, we will pay cash.

What about the terms when you are dealing with REOs? Ah, there is the rub. Are you going to have to pay cash? Are you going to have to qualify for a new loan? Are you going to have a combination of cash and new financing? Will the lender selling you the REO make you a great deal on the interest rate if you get a loan from that lender?

Pre-Foreclosure

We are going to take you through one of our deals. This deal started out in pre-foreclosure. We found a property listed with a broker in our target area. We called on the sign and spoke to the listing agent. She informed us that the owners were very motivated. We liked hearing that.

They were two months behind in their loan payments. The owners were in pre-foreclosure. The agent then told us a separation had occurred between the husband and wife. A divorce was imminent. We liked hearing that even better.

We began working with the owners. We pursued the property through the posting of the notice of default. We were unable to make a deal. We went to the foreclosure sale on the courthouse steps.

We felt the price at which the lender made the credit bid was too high. So did the other investors at the foreclosure sale. No one else bid. The lender had no alternative but to take the property back.

While real estate lenders are professional sellers, sometimes their own bureaucracy gets in the way of them making an effective deal. We did wind up finally making a deal with the lender after the property became an REO. But we are getting ahead of ourselves. First things first.

Working with the Owner The first thing we get from the owner in pre-foreclosure is an *owner authorization to lender for release of borrower information.* We will show you the actual authorization form we use. We will provide blank spaces rather than names in this and the other forms so you can use the forms in your own deals.

We want to speak to the lender directly. This establishes a *contact* between the lender and us. Usually there is one person in the REO department who is assigned to a particular property. If not, we recommend you ask to speak with the same person every time. We didn't realize how important this contact would be until much later.

OWNER AUTHORIZATION TO LENDER FOR RELEASE OF BORROWER INFORMATION

Date: ___________

To Whom It May Concern:

I (We), _______________ (Owner's Name(s)) do authorize the release of my (our) loan information, loan # ______ for the mutual benefit of all parties to ______________ (Investor) and/or ____________ (Investor).

Sincerely,

_________________ (Borrower's Name(s)) __________________

The second thing we get from the owner in pre-foreclosure is an *owner authorization to investor for property access.* We want to be able to get into the property without having to wait for the agent or owner to meet us. In this case, as with many foreclosures, the owners had moved out of the property.

OWNER AUTHORIZATION TO INVESTOR FOR PROPERTY ACCESS

Date: ___________

To Whom It May Concern:

I (We), _________________________________ (Owner's Name(s))

do authorize the ____________________________ (Investor) and/or

_______________________________ (Investor) to access my (our) property at ______________________________.

I (We) have given this authorization to _____________________ so they may show prospective partners and/or investors the property in order to complete funding of our sale.

I (We) have given _____________________ special instructions on how to gain entrance to the property. This authorization for access to my (our) property to ______________________ and/or __________ begins today and extends through _________ (Date).

Signed

______________________ (Owner)

______________________ (Owner)

We next present the owner a *letter of intent to purchase.* We are getting our initial agreement with the owner down on paper. This gives us a written basis of understanding on how the deal will proceed. Again, we give you our actual letter of intent to purchase from this deal.

LETTER OF INTENT TO PURCHASE
CONFIDENTIAL & PRIVILEGED

Date: ___________

This is a letter of intent for seller to sell and buyer to buy from seller ______________________ (property address) for ______________ (net dollars) to seller. This intent to purchase is contingent upon buyer and buyer's attorney approval of the results of: 1. Conversation with seller's lender(s). 2. Conversation with listing broker. 3. Preliminary Title Report.

Closing is to be expedited upon removal of all above contingencies and attorney approval of release of funds for funding this transaction will occur on the next business day. Buyer's attorney is ___________.

Possession of property is to be given to buyer immediately upon acceptance by seller of this letter of intent to purchase. Buyer retains first right of refusal in the event seller receives and accepts any other offers.

If any of the above contingencies or approvals cannot be fulfilled to the satisfaction of the buyer and buyer's attorney, buyer will terminate this intent to purchase the next business day upon dissatisfaction or disapproval. Possession will then be immediately released back to the seller.

Seller accepts costs that buyer is already incurring as consideration for this agreement. This agreement may be assigned by buyer to expedite closing.

______________________	______________________
(Buyer)	(Seller)
______________________	______________________
(Buyer)	(Seller)

Working with the Lender When we contact the lender in the preforeclosure phase, we are looking for two things. First, we want to establish a contact with someone working for the lender. Second, we want something in writing from the lender so we know where we stand moneywise with what the lender thinks is owed. This is called a *payoff quote schedule.*

Payoff Quote Schedule

Principal	$81,057.19
Interest	$ 3,720.37
Late Charges	$ 828.63
Returned Check Fee	$ 100.00
Foreclosure Expense	$ 1,000.00
Attorney Fee and Collection Cost	$ 855.00
Legal Fee	$ 200.00
Foreclosure Cost	$ 502.30
Foreclosure Fee	$ 549.29
Property Valuation Fee	$ 234.00
Property Inspection Fee	$ 7.75
Payoff Quote Fee	$ 10.00
Escrow Advance	$ 3,944.60
Total Amount Due	$92,989.13

Is this an incredible list or what? Why is there a *foreclosure expense* for $1,000, a *foreclosure cost* for $502.30, and a *foreclosure fee* for

$549.29? What are the differences between a foreclosure expense, a foreclosure cost, and a foreclosure fee? Only the lender knows. We think it is padding the bill.

In the nickel-and-dime category, how about the *property inspection fee* for $7.75 and the *payoff quote fee* for $10? Someone drove past the property, and the bank charged a fee. And did you catch the returned check fee for $100? Guess how many returned checks we are talking about. Two!

What is important about the *payoff quote schedule* is that it becomes the basis for the lender's credit bid at the foreclosure sale. In fact this is very close to the actual credit bid this lender made at the foreclosure sale.

Try as we might, we could not get this lender to budge in negotiations during this pre-foreclosure phase. We did not want to pay anywhere near $93,000 for this property. We couldn't find anyone else who wanted to pay that much for the property either.

Because the property was vacant, we were able to bring five different investor groups through it in a week's time. All were in the buy, fix, and flip business. This property definitely needed fixing. We had estimates from these five investor groups from a down-and-dirty $10,000 quick fix to $30,000 to $35,000 to do it right.

We also had prices that the investors would pay for the property in its *as-is* condition that ranged from $70,000 to $85,000. Surprisingly enough, the investor who said he would only put $10,000 into the property to fix it was the same investor who would only pay $70,000 for the property!

The retail value of the property fixed up would be $125,000. If you do the math, it doesn't make sense. Once you pay the lender $93,000 for the property and spend $35,000 to fix it, you are already upside down in the deal. You would have to sell the property at above the retail price of $125,000 just to break even. That was not very likely to happen. We told our contact person with the lender to forget about it.

Upside-Down Deal

Retail Value	$125,000
Lender Payoff	$ 93,000
Fix-Up Costs	$ 35,000
Loss	($ 3,000)

Foreclosure Sale

Needless to say, this property went to the foreclosure sale. The lender made the credit bid of $93,567.23. No one else bid. The trustee awarded the lender a trustee's deed. The lender now owned the property.

The next day we called our contact person at the lender. We asked what the REO department was going to sell the property for. He told us it was going to list the property with a real estate broker for $85,000. He also told us that the price was negotiable!

The price had dropped over $8,000 in one day. So much for getting a good deal at the foreclosure sale! But we already told you that there are deals to be had once a property goes from the foreclosure sale unsold back to the lender as an REO.

REO Offer

This property had now become a saga for us. We had found it in the pre-foreclosure phase. We had tried to put together a deal with the owners. We were successful in getting the owners to work with us for zero net dollars to them. They had no equity in the property. They just wanted our help in walking away from the property.

Our deal with the owners was contingent on working something out with the lender. We were going to flip the property to another real estate investor. We were trying to negotiate the lender down on its loan payoff so there would be some room for us to make a profit. When the lender wouldn't come off the $93,000 payoff, we couldn't make a deal in the pre-foreclosure phase.

We now made an offer of $70,000 all cash for the property. We didn't want to buy the property for $70,000. We wanted to control the property for $70,000. We were not interested in coming up with $70,000 cash. We would leave that to the investor to whom we assigned our contract.

We submitted our offer through our contact person in the REO department. Our offering price wasn't a big bone of contention. The lender simply countered at $80,000. We countered their counteroffer with $73,900, and they accepted.

Our Offer

Lender List Price	$85,000
Our Offer	$70,000
Lender Counteroffer	$80,000
Our Counteroffer	$73,900

However, the lender was unwilling to allow us to assign our contract. We felt we would be able to work out an acceptable price to another investor. If we couldn't get the lender to allow us to assign our contract, then we would have no deal.

The Unassignable Contract It has been our experience that there is no such thing as an unassignable contract. But the toughest contracts to assign are the ones from lenders after they have foreclosed on a loan and are reselling a property.

REO properties are the source of some of our most profitable inventory. However, lenders are just as hoodwinked as the rest of us when it comes to listening to attorneys. They allow their attorneys to put the dumbest things in their REO contracts. Remember, our position on any contract is that the purpose of the contract is to communicate.

Real estate attorneys, just like other attorneys, make money by keeping people from communicating. The following is actual verbiage taken from the lender's REO contract that their attorneys included.

REO REAL ESTATE CONTRACT

"Buyer shall neither assign its rights nor delegate its obligations hereunder without obtaining Seller's prior written consent, which may be withheld in Seller's sole discretion. In no event shall an assignment relieve Buyer from its obligations under this Contract. Any other purported or attempted assignment or delegation without obtaining Seller's prior written consent shall be void and of no effect."

Needless to say, this paragraph was unacceptable to us. How did we get around this affront to our investor sensibilities? Did we get the lender's prior written consent before we wrote an offer? No, we did not. Our contact person gave us a clue.

We wrote the offer as trustees of a trust. As such, we were speaking the language the lender could understand. We did not know when we wrote the offer which trust was actually going to buy the property. The lender accepted our offer as Chantal Carey or Bill Carey, trustees and/or assigns. We assigned the lender's unassignable contract within seven days after our offer was accepted for $79,900.

While this was a lot of work for the relatively small amount of money we made, we were happy. We had tried so hard to make this deal work at each of the four phases of the foreclosure process. To finally have something work in the last phase was very gratifying for us.

Our Profit

Sales Price	$79,900
Purchase Price	$73,900
Our Profit	$ 6,000

We must say that dealing with REO lenders and their attorneys is very difficult. You must legitimately be a trustee before you can write and present contracts as one. We do not recommend this technique if you are just starting out in the foreclosure business.

For those of you who are more advanced or are trustees of trusts and want to consult with us for more information, contact us through our e-mail address, thetrustee@hotmail.com. You must fully identify yourself, or we will not open the e-mail or respond to it.

In the next chapter we will talk about the paperwork, escrow, and title insurance involved in the foreclosure arena. We admonish people to never buy real estate without checking the property title. This can be especially important when you are buying foreclosures. There are exceptions to our rule.

We do know of an investor, for example, who bids on properties on the courthouse steps and does no preliminary research on either the condition of the title or the property. After he wins a bid, he goes inside the courthouse and checks the condition of the title. At the same time he has a partner do a drive-by inspection of the property.

He takes advantage of the two-hour window the foreclosing trustee allows for the winning bidder to produce the cash or cashier's checks. If the property looks like a bomb, he backs out of the deal. If he discovers problems too great for him to handle with the title to the property, he backs out of the deal.

CHAPTER 18

Paperwork, Closing, and Title Insurance

Paperwork

There are no oral agreements in real estate. Everything must be in writing. Once you have written a contract, you have to present it to the seller. By presenting your offer correctly, you have a better chance that your deal will be accepted.

We will show you how to write an offer that will get you a great deal while, at the same time, protect you from winding up in a lousy deal. We will show you how to present your offer in such a way that the seller will see the advantage for him- or herself in accepting your offer.

Writing Your Offer

Technically, you can agree to buy someone's property, and they can agree to sell it to you without a written agreement. *But* if a dispute arises between you and the seller and you wind up in front of a judge, the case will be thrown out as soon as the judge discovers there is no written agreement.

Every state has a statute of frauds that says for a real estate contract to be valid it *must* be in writing. If there is no writing, there is no validity. If there is no validity, there is no contract. Especially in the foreclosure arena, protect yourself by having everything in writing.

CoCa CoLa Besides the requirement that for a real estate contract to be valid it must be in writing, the contract must meet four other requirements. We call this the CoCa CoLa test. We are not promoting or advertising a soft drink but are using CoCa CoLa as a memory aid. Once you understand the four requirements for a valid contract, you will always use the CoCa CoLa test to make sure all the requirements are present.

Consent: There must be mutual consent between the parties to the real estate contract. The parties have to agree about the wording and conditions written in the contract.

Capacity: The parties to the real estate contract must have the capacity to enter into the contract. This means the parties have to be of sound mind (competent) and of legal age (18 in most states). There are some exceptions to the age requirement, such as being married, or being married and then divorced, being in the military, or being an emancipated minor.

Consideration: This is anything of value that influences a person to enter into a real estate contract. It could be money, a deed, a service, an item of personal property, an act (including the payment of money), or a promise (including the promise to pay on a loan). If the consideration is an act or service, that act or service must be performed after the parties enter into the contract. Typically, consideration accompanies the contract in the form of a promissory note or check. Without consideration, the contract is not valid.

Lawful: For the real estate contract to be valid, the promises made between the parties and the consideration given must be legal.

Types of Contracts There are many types of real estate contracts. We are going to show you the four contracts we use for our own real estate investing. The purpose of the contract is to communicate. We believe the simpler the contract, the better the communication between the parties to the contract.

Letter of Intent A letter of intent is our homage to the original one-page real estate purchase contract. You can write anything you want to convey your intent to the seller that you are interested in purchasing the property. A letter of intent is not technically a valid contract, but it does meet our requirement that a contract communicate.

To The Owners of 711 Lucky Street, Oceanside, California:

3/11/05

We intend to make a cash offer on your property within the next 24 hours. In the event you receive another offer before we have had an opportunity to present our offer, we request you give us the first right of refusal and allow us to present our offer before you accept any other offer.

Sincerely,

Chantal & Bill

Option Contract An option contract goes beyond a letter of intent. More than conveying your intent to buy a property, an option contract says you are buying the property within a certain time frame. Also, you will commit funds in the form of an option fee or option money—basically, a deposit—to keep the option open.

Once the option has been agreed to, only the buyer can exercise the option. The seller can't back out of the deal if the buyer exercises the option. The buyer can back out of the deal and not be sued for specific performance.

Purchase Contract A purchase contract is the basic agreement between you and the seller for purchasing the property. Many variations of purchase contracts exist. You can check with local Realtors or title insurance companies to obtain a copy of the type of purchase contracts used in your area. We have included a standard purchase contract in Appendix C.

Purchase contracts have been designed to have standard writing—a boilerplate—to be used in all types of transactions. The blank lines and spaces in the contract are to be used by you to customize your particular deal. We recommend you always stipulate that your offer is contingent on the approval of your money partners.

Remember, regardless of the type of purchase contract you use, the purpose of the contract is to communicate. The more straightforwardly the purchase contract states your intentions to the seller, the easier it will be for the seller to understand what you are trying to do with your offer. If the seller understands what you are trying to do with your offer, then it is more likely he or she will be predisposed to accept your offer. In other words, the simpler your purchase contract is, the better.

Assignment A real estate assignment allows you to take any contract and make Quick Cash by assigning your interest in the contract to someone else for a fee. The important part is for you to write every real estate contract with the clause "and/or assigns" as part of your name in the buyer's name section of the contract. This will give you the right and ability to assign a contract of whatever kind to another buyer for a fee.

Presenting Your Offer

The purpose of presenting your offer is to have the seller accept it. There are three responses a seller can have to your offer. The seller can accept your offer. The seller can counter your offer. The seller can reject your offer. If the seller accepts, you have a contract. If the seller counters, you have something to work with. If the seller rejects and says no, you may be at a dead end. You don't want the seller to say no.

You begin building rapport the moment you start an interaction with a person. We have found that smiling at, being respectful toward, and being complimentary to a seller builds rapport. You also have to be energetic and upbeat when you interact with a seller to instill the belief that you can get a real estate transaction done.

We go into every transaction with a seller with a win-win attitude. We want the seller to win, and we want to win. You will find that as a real estate investor, getting a good deal is easy. You just have to ask. When we make an offer, we want to get a good deal. We find that when we get a good deal, we are solving a problem for the seller—especially the seller in the foreclosure process. That makes it a win-win for the seller and for us.

Where to Present Your Offer Always present your offer at the seller's kitchen table. Arrange to sit at the head of the table with your back to an outside wall. You want the seller's attention focused on you, not what is going on in the rest of the house.

By presenting your offer at the kitchen table, you convey that this is a business situation. If you present the offer in the living room, it conveys a social interaction. Ask that televisions and radios be turned off. Do not accept an offer of food. Accepting an offer of a beverage (nonalcoholic) is fine.

When to Present Your Offer Present your offer within 72 hours of seeing the property for the first time so you will convey a sense of urgency and interest to the seller. Sellers want to know if you are a serious buyer. Serious buyers take action in a timely manner. When you are working with the owner in pre-foreclosure, we recommend you make your offer after you make the foreclosure options presentation.

Closing

In our Quick Cash in foreclosures system, you may wind up receiving money directly from another real estate investor without going to a closing. You could be flipping a property before the closing. You could be assigning a purchase contract or an option contract to another investor, who will then go to a closing with a seller. You will get a feel for when you will go to a closing and when you will not.

Escrow

Understanding how the escrow closes can make you comfortable with a process many buyers and sellers find very confusing. *Escrow* is a type of closing in which you and the seller deposit money and/or documents with a neutral third party—the escrow holder. You and the seller give the escrow holder instructions to hold and disburse documents and funds after certain conditions are met.

An escrow is complete when all conditions listed in the escrow instructions are met and all acts specified in the instructions are performed. When an escrow is complete, the escrow holder disburses the funds and documents to close the escrow.

In its simplest format an escrow would have the buyer put the money in the escrow account at the opening of escrow. The seller would take the money out of the escrow at the closing of the escrow. The seller would put the deed to the property in escrow at the opening of the escrow. The buyer would take the deed to the property out of the escrow at the closing of the escrow.

Many things are occurring during the escrow period: termite inspections, physical inspections, money partner inspections, geological inspections, title searches, procuring hazard insurance, obtaining financing, preparing loan documents, calculating closing costs, preparing deeds, and so on.

Opening an Escrow Consider choosing an escrow holder who is willing to take the time to explain what is happening and what you need to do. Choose a company that is located a convenient distance from where you live, so you can sign and deliver documents or money easily.

Depending on your area, the party that acts as the escrow holder can include independent escrow companies, escrow departments of lending institutions, title insurance companies, real estate brokers, and real estate attorneys. You may find that your area does a closing with an attorney rather than conducting an escrow.

The Buyer's Day The day the escrow closes is considered the *buyer's day.* What this means is that all the prorations of property taxes, hazard insurance, mortgage interest, and property rents are figured on this day.

Let's say the escrow closes on the 14th day of the month. The seller is responsible for paying the property taxes, hazard insurance, and mortgage interest through the 13th day of the month. If the property is receiving rental income, the seller is entitled to receive a prorated share of the monthly rent through the 13th day of the month. This is because rents are paid in advance, usually on the first day of the month.

The buyer is responsible for paying the property taxes, hazard insurance, and mortgage interest starting on the 14th day of the month. If the property is receiving rental income, the buyer is entitled to receive a prorated share of the monthly rent from the 14th day of the month until the end of the month.

Closing Statement Once the escrow closes, a *closing statement* is prepared by the escrow holder. The closing statement is set up as a debit and credit accounting. The purchase price appears as a credit to the seller and a debit to the buyer. Any rental security deposits will be credited to the buyer and debited to the seller. Everything else will be prorated as a debit and a credit to the seller and buyer, respectively, based on the day of closing.

Title Insurance

If you buy property, get title insurance. *Never buy property without title insurance.* What is title insurance? *Title insurance* is a policy of insurance issued to you by a title company on completion of the final title search, which protects your title to property against claims made in the future based on circumstances in the past.

Title insurance is especially important when you are investing in foreclosures. Liens and encumbrances against the property title tend to mushroom during the foreclosure process. Besides the foreclosing lender, there may be tax liens, lawsuits, and other creditors with interests against the title to the property.

Title Search

A *title search* is an examination of information recorded on a property, or the owner of the property, at the county recorder's office in the county in which the property is located. The examination verifies that the property will have no outstanding liens or claims against it to adversely affect a buyer or lender when the title to the property is transferred to a new buyer or pledged as collateral for a real estate loan.

When you are buying property, especially a foreclosure property, it is always a good idea to get a preliminary title report from a title insurance company. The preliminary title report is usually produced by the title company during the escrow or closing. The purpose of the preliminary report is to make everyone—buyer, seller, lender, escrow holder, title company—aware of the condition of the title involved in the transaction.

Owner's Policy An owner's policy of title insurance protects the owner of record from claims against the title brought by other parties. If a claim arises and you have title insurance, and any monetary damages are to be paid, the title insurance company will pay them. By the way, the seller or buyer can pay for the owner's policy.

Buyer's Policy A buyer's policy of title insurance protects the buyer of real estate. The buyer's policy is similar to the lender's policy in that it protects the buyer for matters beyond what is in the public record. Although the buyer becomes the owner and is protected by the owner's policy, a buyer may decide to get extended coverage. We recommend getting buyer's coverage any time you are involved in a foreclosure transaction.

Lender's Policy A lender's policy of title insurance protects the real estate lender beyond matters of public record. There may be unrecorded liens against the title. Lenders want to be protected against everything because they have so much money loaned on the property. Typically, the lender makes the buyer who is using the loan proceeds to complete the purchase of the property pay for the lender's title policy.

Conclusion

Congratulations on completing *Quick Cash in Foreclosures.* We know you have a lot of material to digest. Our hope is that we have stimulated your interest in making money in foreclosures.

Our recommendation is for you to go back to the areas that are of the most interest for you. Please reread them. Then get started. Look at property. Schedule an appointment with an owner in pre-foreclosure. Make a foreclosure options presentation.

Write an offer. Flip a property or a contract. Assign something. Control a property with an option. Go to a foreclosure sale. Our point is: Do something! Make some money.

We are always coming up with more creative possibilities for investments and problem solving. So, as we bid you adieu, we have this to say to you: Get creative! Pull a group of people together and contact us for a seminar.

Are you a lone ranger right now? You won't be for long when you start investing in foreclosures. Meanwhile, you can e-mail us for fee-based consulting. We are always open to new possibilities, so let us know if you need a partner. Get out there and do something *now!*

Let us know what did or didn't work for you. We want to hear about your experiences in the foreclosure arena. You can contact us through our publisher, e-mail us at thetrustee@hotmail.com, or write to us at P.O. Box 274, Bedford, TX 76095-0274.

Remember to watch for more of this Win Going In! series. The first book in the series was *The New Path to Real Estate Wealth: Earning Without Owning*. *Quick Cash in Foreclosures* is the second book in the series. The third book will be on investing in tax liens and will come out in the spring of 2005. God bless y'all!

—Bill & Chantal Carey

APPENDIX A

Deeds Chart

G = Grant deed is a deed using the word *grant* in the clause that awards ownership. This written document is used by the grantor (seller) to transfer title to the grantee (buyer). Grant deeds have two implied warranties. One is that the grantor has not previously transferred the title. The other is that the title is free from encumbrances that are not visible to the grantee. This deed also transfers any title acquired by the grantor after delivery of the deed.

W = Warranty deed is a deed in which the grantor (usually the seller) guarantees the title to be in the condition indicated in the deed. The grantor agrees to protect the grantee (usually the buyer) against all claimants to the property.

* = Special deed.

State	*Deeds*	*State*	*Deeds*	*State*	*Deeds*
Alabama	W	Louisiana	W	Oklahoma	G
Alaska	W	Maine	W	Oregon	W
Arizona	G	Maryland	W	Pennsylvania	G
Arkansas	G	Massachusetts	W	Puerto Rico	*
California	G	Michigan	W	Rhode Island	W
Colorado	W	Minnesota	W	South Carolina	G & W
Connecticut	W	Mississippi	W	South Dakota	W
Delaware	G	Missouri	W	Tennessee	W
District of Columbia	G	Montana	G	Texas	G
Florida	W	Nebraska	W	Utah	W
Georgia	W	Nevada	G	Vermont	W

(continued)

(Continued)

State	*Deeds*	*State*	*Deeds*	*State*	*Deeds*
Hawaii	W	New Hampshire	W	Virginia	G
Idaho	W	New Jersey	G & W	Washington	W
Illinois	G & W	New Mexico	W	West Virginia	G
Indiana	W	New York	G	Wisconsin	W
Iowa	W	North Carolina	W	Wyoming	W
Kansas	W	North Dakota	G & W		
Kentucky	W	Ohio	W		

APPENDIX B

Loans Chart

M = Mortgage, a contract by which you promise your property with out giving up possession of the property to secure a loan. You also retain title to the property.

TD = Trust deed, a contract used as a security device for a loan on your property, by which you transfer bare (naked) legal title with the power of sale to a trustee. This transfer is in effect until you have totally paid off the loan. In the meantime you have possession of the property.

*Mortgage preferred; trust deed also valid.

**Trust deed preferred; mortgage also valid.

***Use note to secure debt.

State	*Loans*	*State*	*Loans*	*State*	*Loans*
Alabama	M & TD	Louisiana	M	Oklahoma	M & TD
Alaska	M & TD	Maine	M	Oregon	M & TD
Arizona	M & TD	Maryland	M & TD	Pennsylvania	M
Arkansas	M	Massachusetts	M	Puerto Rico	M
California	TD	Michigan	M	Rhode Island	M
Colorado	TD	Minnesota	M	South Carolina	M & TD
Connecticut	M	Mississippi	M & TD**	South Dakota	M
Delaware	M	Missouri	TD	Tennessee	TD
District of Columbia	TD	Montana	M & TD*	Texas	TD
Florida	M & TD	Nebraska	M & TD	Utah	M & TD
Georgia	***	Nevada	M & TD	Vermont	M
Hawaii	M	New Hampshire	M	Virginia	M & TD*

(continued)

(Continued)

State	*Loans*	*State*	*Loans*	*State*	*Loans*
Idaho	M & TD	New Jersey	M	Washington	M & TD
Illinois	M & TD	New Mexico	M & TD	West Virginia	TD
Indiana	M & TD	New York	M	Wisconsin	M
Iowa	M & TD	North Carolina	M & TD	Wyoming	M & TD
Kansas	M	North Dakota	M & TD		
Kentucky	M & TD*	Ohio	M		

APPENDIX C

Contracts

PURCHASE CONTRACT FOR REAL ESTATE AND DEPOSIT RECEIPT

This is meant to be a legally binding agreement. Read it carefully.

City:______________________ State:_________________ Date:_______________

Received from ______________________________, the buyer, the sum of $__________

shown by ☐ cash, ☐ cashier's check, ☐ personal check, or ☐ ___________________

payable to ____

to be held uncashed until this offer is accepted as deposit toward the purchase price of

____ Dollars ($_______________)

for the purchase of property located in the state of __________________________________,

county of _________________________, city of___________________________,

and known as ____.

CAPTIONS: The headings and captions in this document are to make reference easy and are not intended as a part of this agreement.

1. **FIXTURES:** All permanently installed fixtures, fittings, and plantings that are attached to the property or for which special openings were made, as well as their controls, if any, are included in the purchase price, including ____

   ____

   except ____.

2. **PERSONAL PROPERTY:** The following items of personal property, free of liens and without warranty are included: ____

   ____

3. **PROPERTY CONDITION:** Seller guarantees, that through the date seller makes possession available to buyer

   A. The property and improvements, including grounds and landscaping, shall be maintained in the same condition as on the date of acceptance of the offer;

   B. The roof is free of all known leaks;

   C. All permanently installed fixtures and fittings, as well as their controls, if any, are operative;

   D. Seller shall replace any cracked or broken glass;

   E. And ____

   F. Except ____

   ____

4. **SELLER REPRESENTATION:** Seller guarantees that until the date escrow closes that seller knows of no violation notices of codes, laws, or other regulations issued or filed against the property.

5. **SUPPLEMENTS:** The attached documents are incorporated in this document:

   ☐ ____

   ☐ ____

   ☐ ____

   ☐ ____

(continued)

Buyer and seller acknowledge receiving a duplicate of this page, which is page 1 of ____ pages.

Buyers' initials (______) (______) Sellers' initials (______) (______)

PURCHASE CONTRACT FOR REAL ESTATE AND DEPOSIT RECEIPT

Property known as ____

6. **ESCROW:** Buyer and seller shall deliver signed instructions to ______________________________ ______________________________, the escrow holder, within _____ calendar days of acceptance of the offer. The offer shall provide for closing within ______ calendar days of acceptance. Escrow fees to be paid as follows: ____

____

7. **OCCUPANCY:** Buyer ☐ does ☐ does not intend to occupy property as buyer's primary residence.
8. **POSSESSION:** Possession and occupancy shall be delivered to buyer ☐ on the close of escrow ☐ no later than _____ days after the close of escrow or ☐ ______________________
9. **KEYS:** Seller shall provide keys and/or other means to operate all property locks and alarms, if any, when possession is available to the buyer.
10. **FINANCING:** This agreement depends on the buyer obtaining financing.
    A. DILIGENCE AND GOOD FAITH - Buyer agrees to act with diligence and good faith to obtain all appropriate financing.
    B. DEPOSIT is due on acceptance and is to be deposited into ___________ ______________________________ in the amount of $____________
    C. INCREASED DEPOSIT is due within ____ days of acceptance and is to be deposited into ______________________ in the amount of $____________
    D. DOWN PAYMENT BALANCE is to be deposited into ________________ ________________ on or before ____________ in the amount of $____________
    E. NEW FIRST LOAN - Buyer to apply for, qualify for, and obtain new first loan in the amount of .... $____________
    payable monthly at approximately $________________
    including interest at origination not to exceed ___________ %
    ☐ fixed rate ☐ other ______________________________
    all due ______ years from the date of origination.
    Loan fee at origination not to exceed $________________ .
    Seller agrees to pay a maximum of ____________ FHA/VA discount points.
    Additional terms:______________________________________

    ____

    ____
    F. EXISTING FIRST LOAN - Buyer to ☐ assume ☐ take title subject to an existing first loan with an approximate balance of .... $____________
    payable monthly at $______________ including interest at _________ %
    ☐ fixed rate ☐ other ______________________________
    Fees not to exceed $____________ . Disposition of impound account ___

    ____

    Additional terms: ______________________________________

    ____

    ____

(continued)

Buyer and seller acknowledge receiving a duplicate of this page, which is page 2 of ___ pages.
Buyers' initials (_____) (_____) Sellers' initials (_____) (_____)

PURCHASE CONTRACT FOR REAL ESTATE AND DEPOSIT RECEIPT

Property known as ____

10. FINANCING:

G. NOTE SECURED BY TRUST DEED - Buyer to sign a note secured by a
☐ first ☐ second ☐ third trust deed in the amount of .... $______________
in favor of seller, payable monthly at $_______________ or more
including interest at ________ %
☐ fixed rate ☐ other _________________________________
all due ☐______ years from date of origination or ☐ upon sale or
transfer of the property.
A late charge of $_____________ shall be due on any installment not paid
within ________ days of the date due.
Additional terms: ____
____.

H. NEW SECOND LOAN - Buyer to apply for, qualify for, and obtain new
second loan in the amount of .... $______________
payable monthly at approximately $_____________
including interest at origination not to exceed _________ %
☐ fixed rate ☐ other ____
all due ______ years from date of origination.
Buyer's loan fees not to exceed $__________ .
Seller agrees to pay a maximum of _____________ FHA/VA discount points.
Additional terms:____
____.

I. EXISTING SECOND LOAN - Buyer to ☐ assume ☐ take title subject
to an existing second loan with an approximate balance of .... $______________
payable monthly at $_______________ including interest at ________ %
☐ fixed rate ☐ other ____
Buyers loan fees not to exceed $_____________ .
Additional terms:____
____.

J. OTHER PROVISIONS - If buyer assumes or takes title "subject to" an existing loan, seller shall provide buyer with copies of applicable notes and trust deeds. Buyer is allowed _______ calendar days after receipt of such copies to examine the copies for the features that affect the loan and to notify seller in writing of disapproval. Buyer shall not unreasonably withhold approval. *Failure to notify seller in writing shall conclusively be considered approval.*

K. ADDITIONAL FINANCING TERMS: ______________________________
____
____

L. TOTAL PURCHASE PRICE... $______________

(continued)

Buyer and seller acknowledge receiving a duplicate of this page, which is page 3 of ____ pages.
Buyers' initials (______) (______) Sellers' initials (______) (______)

PURCHASE CONTRACT FOR REAL ESTATE AND DEPOSIT RECEIPT

Property known as ____

11. TITLE: Title is to be free of conditions, easements, encumbrances, liens, restrictions, and rights of record other than the following:

A. Current property taxes;

B. Covenants, conditions, restrictions, and public utility easements of record, if any, if the items do not adversely affect the continuing use of the property for the purposes for which it is currently used, unless the buyer reasonably disapproves in writing within ______ calendar days of receipt of a current preliminary report furnished at ________________ expense; and

C. Seller shall furnish buyer at ______________expense, a ________________________________ policy issued by ____ company, showing title vested in buyer subject only to the above. If seller is unwilling or unable to eliminate any title matter disapproved by buyer as indicated above, the buyer may end this agreement. If seller fails to deliver title as indicated above, buyer may end this agreement. In either case deposit shall be returned to the buyer.

12. VESTING: The title shall vest as follows: ________________________________ ________________________________ unless noted otherwise in the buyer's escrow instructions.

13. PRORATIONS: Association dues, interest, payments on assessments and bonds assumed by buyer, premiums on insurance acceptable to the buyer, property taxes, rents, and ________________ ____ shall be paid current and prorated as of ☐ the day the deed records; or ☐ ____.
Bonds or assessments that are now a lien shall be paid current by seller, payments not yet due to be ☐ assumed by the buyer; ☐ paid in full by the seller, including payments not yet due; or ☐ ____.
County transfer tax, if applicable, shall be paid by ______________ . The ____________________ transfer tax or transfer fee shall be paid by ______________ . Reassessment of the property when ownership changes affects taxes to be paid. A supplemental tax bill may be issued, which shall be paid by the seller for periods before escrow closes and by the buyer for periods after escrow closes. Buyer and seller shall handle between themselves tax bills issued after escrow closes.

14. TAX WITHHOLDING: Under the Foreign Investment in Real Property Tax Act (FIRPTA), buyers of U.S. real property *must* deduct and withhold from the seller's proceeds 10% of the gross sales price unless an exemption applies. States may require that additional money be withheld.

15. OTHER TERMS AND CONDITIONS:

____

____

____

____

____

____

____

16. ATTORNEY'S FEES: In any action, arbitration, or proceeding arising out of this agreement, the prevailing party shall be entitled to reasonable attorney's fees and costs.

(continued)

Buyer and seller acknowledge receiving a duplicate of this page, which is page 4 of ____ pages.
Buyers' initials (______) (______) Sellers' initials (______) (______)

PURCHASE CONTRACT FOR REAL ESTATE AND DEPOSIT RECEIPT

Property known as ____________________

17. ENTIRE CONTRACT:

A. Time is important.

B. All earlier agreements between buyer and seller are made a part of this agreement, which makes up the whole contract. The terms of this contract are intended by buyer and seller as their final agreement about the terms that are included in this contract. The terms of this contract may not be contradicted by evidence of any earlier agreement or any oral contract made at the same time as this written contract.

C. The buyer and seller agree that this contract makes up the complete and exclusive statement of the contract's terms and that no extraneous evidence of any kind may be introduced in any judicial or arbitration proceeding, if any, about this contract.

18. AMENDMENTS:

The buyer and seller may not alter, amend, change, or modify this contract except by further agreement in writing signed by both buyer and seller.

19. OFFER:

A. This makes up an offer to purchase the property described.

B. Unless acceptance is signed by seller and a signed copy is delivered in person, by mail, or facsimile and received by the buyer at the address indicated below within _____ calendar days of the date of this contract, this offer will be considered revoked and the deposit shall be returned.

C. Buyer has read and acknowledges receipt of a copy of this offer.

D. This agreement and any addition or modification relating to this agreement including any photocopy or facsimile of this contract may be signed in two or more counterparts, all of which shall make up one and the same writing.

BUYER:____________________	BUYER:____________________
Address:____________________	Address:____________________
____________________	____________________
Telephone:____________________	Telephone:____________________

ACCEPTANCE

The seller who signed below accepts and agrees to sell the property in the manner indicated below.

☐ On the above terms and conditions. ☐ Subject to the attached counteroffer.

SELLER:____________________	SELLER:____________________
Address:____________________	Address:____________________
____________________	____________________
Telephone:____________________	Telephone:____________________

Buyer and Seller acknowledge receiving a duplicate of this page, which is page 5 of ____ pages.

Buyers' initials (______) (______) Sellers' initials (______) (______)

PURCHASE CONTRACT FOR REAL ESTATE ADDITIONAL TERMS AND CONDITIONS

This is meant to be a legally binding agreement. Read it carefully.

This document contains additional terms and conditions to the Purchase Contract for Real Estate and Deposit Receipt for the purchase of the property located in the state of____________________________,
county of ________________________________, city of ____________________________________,
and known as ____.
This document, when used, is meant to be an addition to the Purchase Contract for Real Estate and Deposit Receipt.

CAPTIONS: The headings and captions in this document are to make reference easy and are not intended as a part of this agreement.

To be included in the agreement items *must* be initialed by both *buyer(s)* and *seller(s)*.

1. PHYSICAL AND GEOLOGICAL INSPECTIONS:

A. Buyer has the right, at buyer's expense, to select a licensed contractor and /or other qualified professional(s) to make inspections of the property for possible environmental hazards.
   - These inspections can include inspections, investigations, tests, and other studies.
   - The inspections can include but are not limited to the fixtures and fittings of the property and controls for the fixtures and fittings, if any; geological conditions; and possible environmental hazards including substances, products, and other conditions.

B. Buyer shall keep the property free and clear of any liens. Buyer shall indemnify and hold seller harmless from all liability, claims, demands, damages, or costs and shall repair all damages to the property arising from the inspections.

C. Buyer shall make all claims about defects in the condition of the property that adversely affect continuing use of the property for the purposes for which it is currently being used or as ____ in writing, supported by written reports, if any. The buyer shall cause these documents to be delivered to the seller, within the number of calendar days specified below of the acceptance of the offer. For all types of physical inspections, except geological inspections, the documents shall be delivered within ______ calendar days. For geological inspections the documents shall be delivered within ______ calendar days.

D. Buyer shall provide seller with copies, at no cost to the seller, of all reports about the property obtained by the buyer.

E. Buyer may cancel this agreement if any of these reports disclose conditions or information unacceptable to the buyer, which the seller is unable or unwilling to correct.

F. Seller shall make the property available for all inspections.

G. *Buyer's failure to notify seller in writing regarding the above shall conclusively be considered approval.*

Initials: Buyers: _______ _______ **Sellers:** _______ _______

(continued)

Buyer and seller acknowledge receiving a duplicate of this page, which is page 1 of ___ pages.
Buyers' initials (______) (______) Sellers' initials (______) (______)

PURCHASE CONTRACT FOR REAL ESTATE ADDITIONAL TERMS AND CONDITIONS

Property known as ____

2. PEST CONTROL

A. Within _____ calendar days of acceptance of the offer, seller shall furnish buyer at the expense of ☐ buyer, ☐ seller, a current written report of an inspection by ______________________ ___________________________, a licensed pest control operator. This inspection shall be of one or more of the following areas: ☐ the main building, ☐ detached garage(s) or carport(s), if any, and ☐ the following other structure(s) on the property:_________________ ____.

B. If either Buyer or Seller request it, the report shall separately identify each recommendation for corrective action as follows:
Type 1: Infestation or infection that is evident.
Type 2: Conditions present that are considered likely to lead to infestation or infection.

C. If no infestation or infection by wood-destroying pests or organisms is found, the report shall include a written certification that on the inspection date no evidence of active infestation or infection was found.

D. All work recommended to correct conditions described as type 1 shall be at the expense of the ☐ seller. ☐ buyer.

E. All work recommended to correct conditions described as type 2, if requested by the buyer, shall be at the expense of the ☐ seller. ☐ buyer.

F. The repairs shall be done with good workmanship and materials of comparable quality to the originals. These repairs shall include repairs and the replacement of materials removed for repairs. Buyer and seller understand that exact restoration of appearance or cosmetic items following all such repairs is not included.

G. Funds for work agreed to be performed after escrow closes shall be held in escrow and paid on receipt of written certification that the inspected property is now free of active infestation or infection.

H. If the report recommends inspection of inaccessible areas, buyer has the option to accept and approve the report, or within ______ calendar days from receipt of the report to request in writing that a further inspection be made. *Buyer's failure to notify seller in writing of such request shall conclusively be considered approval of the report.*
If additional inspection recommends type 1 or 2 corrective measures, such work shall be done at the expense of whoever is designated in section 2D and/or 2E above. If no infestation is found, the cost of inspection, entry, and closing of inaccessible areas shall be at buyer's expense.

I. Other ____
____
____
____
____

Initials: Buyers: _______ _______ Sellers: _______ _______

(continued)

Buyer and seller acknowledge receiving a duplicate of this page, which is page 2 of ____ pages.
Buyers' initials (______) (______) Sellers' initials (______) (______)

PURCHASE CONTRACT FOR REAL ESTATE ADDITIONAL TERMS AND CONDITIONS

Property known as ____

3. ENERGY CONSERVATION RETROFIT:

If applicable, governmental laws require that the property be made to conform to minimum energy conservation standards as a condition of sale or transfer; ☐ buyer, ☐ seller shall comply with and pay for the work necessary to meet these requirements. If the seller must bring the property into compliance, the seller may, where the law permits, authorize escrow to credit the buyer with enough funds to cover the cost of the retrofit.

Initials: Buyers: _______ _______ Sellers: _______ _______

4. FLOOD HAZARD AREA DISCLOSURE:

The buyer is informed that the property is located in a "Special Flood Hazard Area" as set forth on a Federal Emergency Management Agency (FEMA) "Flood Insurance Rate Map" (FIRM) or "Flood Hazard Boundary Map" (FHBM).

A. The law requires that, to obtain financing on most structures located in a "Special Flood Hazard Area," lenders require flood insurance where the property or its attachments are security for a loan.

B. No representation is made by the seller as to the legal or economic effects of the National Flood Insurance Program and related legislation.

Initials: Buyers: _______ _______ Sellers: _______ _______

5. HOME PROTECTION PLAN:

Home protection plans may provide additional protection and benefit to seller and buyer.
The buyer and seller agree to include a home protection plan to be issued by __________________

____

at a cost not to exceed $_____________ to be paid for by ☐ Buyer, ☐ Seller.

Initials: Buyers: _______ _______ Sellers: _______ _______

6. CONDOMINIUM/PLANNED UNIT DEVELOPMENT (PUD):

A. The property is a ☐ condominium ☐ planned unit development (PUD) designated as unit ___________ and ________ parking spaces, and an undivided interest in community areas, and ____.
The current monthly assessment charge, fees, or dues by the homeowner's association or other governing body is $______________.

B. As soon as practical, seller shall provide buyer with copies of any documents required by law including the articles of incorporation; claims; covenants, conditions, and restrictions; current rules and regulations; litigations; most current financial statement; and pending special assessments.

C. Buyer is allowed _____ calendar days from receipt to review these documents. If documents disclose conditions or information unacceptable to buyer, buyer may cancel this agreement.

D. *Buyer's failure to notify seller in writing shall conclusively be considered approval.*

Initials: Buyers: _______ _______ Sellers: _______ _______

(continued)

Buyer and seller acknowledge receiving a duplicate of this page, which is page 3 of ____ pages.

Buyers' initials (______) (______) Sellers' initials (______) (______)

PURCHASE CONTRACT FOR REAL ESTATE
ADDITIONAL TERMS AND CONDITIONS

Property known as ____

7. LIQUIDATED DAMAGES: If buyer fails to complete purchase of the property because of any default of the buyer, seller is released from obligation to sell the property to buyer. Seller may then proceed against buyer on any claim or remedy that seller may have in equity or law. By initialing this paragraph, buyer and seller agree that seller shall retain the deposit as liquidated damages. **NOTICE: Funds deposited in trust accounts or in escrow are not released automatically in the event of a dispute. Release of funds requires written agreement of the parties, judicial decision, or arbitration.**

Initials: Buyers: _______ _______ Sellers: _______ _______

8. DISPUTE ARBITRATION: Any dispute or claim in law or equity arising out of this contract or any resulting transaction shall be decided by neutral binding arbitration in accordance with the rules of the American Arbitration Association and not by state law except as the law provides for judicial review of arbitration proceedings. Judgment upon the award rendered by the arbitrator shall be entered in any court having jurisdiction over the case. The parties shall have the right of discovery.

The following matters are excluded from arbitration:

A. A judicial or nonjudicial foreclosure or other action or proceeding to enforce a deed of trust, mortgage, or a real property sales contract.
B. An unlawful detainer action.
C. The filing or enforcement of a mechanic's lien.
D. Any matter that is within the jurisdiction of a probate court, and/or
E. Bodily injury, wrongful death, hidden or evident defects, and actions to which civil codes apply. The filing of a judicial action to enable the recording of a notice of pending action, for order of attachment, receivership, injunction, or other temporary remedies, shall not be a waiver of the right to arbitrate under this provision.

NOTICE: Agreement to this provision is voluntary. If you refuse to submit to arbitration after agreeing to this provision, you may be forced to arbitrate. By initialing below you are

A. Agreeing to have any dispute arising out of the matters included in this "Dispute Arbitration" provision decided by neutral arbitration as provided by your state law.
B. Giving up any rights you may possess to have the dispute litigated in a court or jury trial.
C. Giving up your judicial rights to discovery and appeal, unless those rights are specifically included in the "Dispute Arbitration" provision.

We have read and understood this provision to arbitrate a dispute, and we agree to this provision.

Initials: Buyers: _______ _______ Sellers: _______ _______

Receipt of this document is acknowledged:

Date:________________ Seller: ______________________________
Date:________________ Seller: ______________________________
Date:________________ Buyer: ______________________________
Date:________________ Buyer: ______________________________

Buyer and seller acknowledge receiving a duplicate of this page, which is page 4 of ___ pages.

Buyers' initials (______) (______) Sellers' initials (______) (______)

CONTRACT CHANGES AND ADDITIONS

This is meant to be a legally binding agreement. Read it carefully.

The following changes and additions are united with and made a part of the Real Estate Purchase Contract and Receipt for Deposit that is dated ______________________________
between ____, the seller, and
____, the buyer, on the property
known as ____.

The changes and additions are as follows:

____

____

____

____

____

____

____

____

____

____

____

____

____

____

____

____

____

____

____

____

____

____

____

____

____

Receipt of this notice is acknowledged:

Date:____________________ Seller:______________________________

Date:____________________ Seller:______________________________

Date:____________________ Buyer:______________________________

Date:____________________ Buyer:______________________________

Buyer and seller acknowledge receiving a duplicate of this page, which is page ____ of ____ pages.

Buyers' initials (______) (______) Sellers' initials (______) (______)

COUNTEROFFER

This is meant to be a legally binding agreement. Read it carefully.

This counteroffer to the Real Estate Purchase Contract and Receipt for Deposit on the property known as____ is dated _______________________. In this contract _______________________________ is referred to as the buyer and _______________________________is referred to as the seller.

Seller accepts all of the conditions and terms in the agreement noted above with the following changes:

____
____
____
____
____
____
____
____
____
____
____
____
____
____
____
____
____
____
____

The seller retains the right to continue to offer the property described for sale. The seller also retains the right to agree to any offer acceptable to seller at any time before the personal acceptance by seller of a copy of this counteroffer, properly accepted and signed by the buyer. *Accept* as used in this document, includes delivery in person, by mail, or by facsimile.

If this counteroffer is not accepted on or before the date of ___________________________at _____A.M./P.M., the counteroffer shall be considered canceled and the deposit shall be returned to the buyer. The seller's agreement to another offer shall cancel this counteroffer. This counteroffer and any addition or modification relating to it, including any photocopy or facsimile of it, may be signed in two or more duplicates, all of which will make up the same writing. Acceptance of a copy is acknowledged.

Date:______________________ Seller:____________________________________

Time:______________________ Seller:____________________________________

(continued)

Buyer and seller acknowledge receiving a duplicate of this page, which is page 1 of ____ pages.

Buyers' initials (______) (______) Sellers' initials (______) (______)

COUNTEROFFER

This is meant to be a legally binding agreement. Read it carefully.

Property known as ____

☐ The undersigned buyer accepts the above counteroffer without addition or modification, OR
☐ The undersigned buyer accepts the above counteroffer with the following additions or modifications:

If the following additions or modifications are not accepted and a copy properly accepted and signed is not personally delivered to the buyer or ______________________, the agent obtaining the offer, on or before ________________ at _____A.M./P.M., the counteroffer shall be considered canceled and the deposit shall be returned to the buyer. Acceptance of a copy is acknowledged.

____
____
____
____
____
____
____
____
____

Date:______________________ Buyer:______________________________
Time:______________________ Buyer:______________________________

Acceptance of a signed copy on________________________ at _______ A.M./P.M. by seller is acknowledged.

IF BUYER MADE ADDITIONS OR MODIFICATIONS ABOVE, THE FOLLOWING IS REQUIRED:
Seller accepts buyer's additions or modifications to seller's counteroffer. The seller agrees to sell on the above terms and conditions. Seller acknowledges receipt of a copy.

Date:______________________ Seller:______________________________
Time:______________________ Seller:______________________________

Buyer and seller acknowledge receiving a duplicate of this page, which is page 2 of ____ pages.
Buyers' initials (______) (______) Sellers' initials (______) (______)

CONDITION(S) RELEASE

This is meant to be a legally binding agreement. Read it carefully.

This addition is a part of the Purchase Contract for Real Estate and Deposit Receipt that is dated ________________________ between ____(seller) and ____(buyer) on the property known as ____.

Seller has the right to continue to offer subject property for sale.

If the seller accepts a later written offer, in accordance with the named buyer's rights, the buyer shall have _____hours ________days following receiving notice to remove and renounce in writing the following condition(s): ____
____
____
____
____
____
____
____

In the event buyer shall fail to remove the condition(s) within the above time limit, the Purchase Contract for Real Estate and Deposit Receipt and this agreement shall end and become voidable and the buyer's deposit shall be returned to the buyer.

This Condition(s) Release shall be considered to have been received by buyer when buyer, or buyer's agent, has received notice by delivery in person or by certified mail addressed to __________________ ____.

If notice is given by mail, the buyer has until 6:00 P.M. of the third day following the date of mailing (unless the notice provides another time), to deliver to the seller the buyer's written agreement to remove and void the condition(s).

The person or persons signing below acknowledge receiving a copy of this document.

RECEIPT FOR DELIVERY IN PERSON

Date:______________________ Seller:____
Date:______________________ Seller:____

Date:______________________ Buyer: ____
Date:______________________ Buyer: ____

Buyer and seller acknowledge receiving a duplicate of this page, which is page 1 of ____ pages.
Buyers' initials (______) (______) Sellers' initials (______) (______)

PROMISSORY NOTES

_______________, _______

I(we) hereby promise to pay to the order of _______________

payable at _______________, _______

in the amount of _______________ ***Dollars*** **$** _______

with interest in the amount of _______________ *per cent (_____%) per annum*

due on or before _______________, _______

Signature _______________

199120

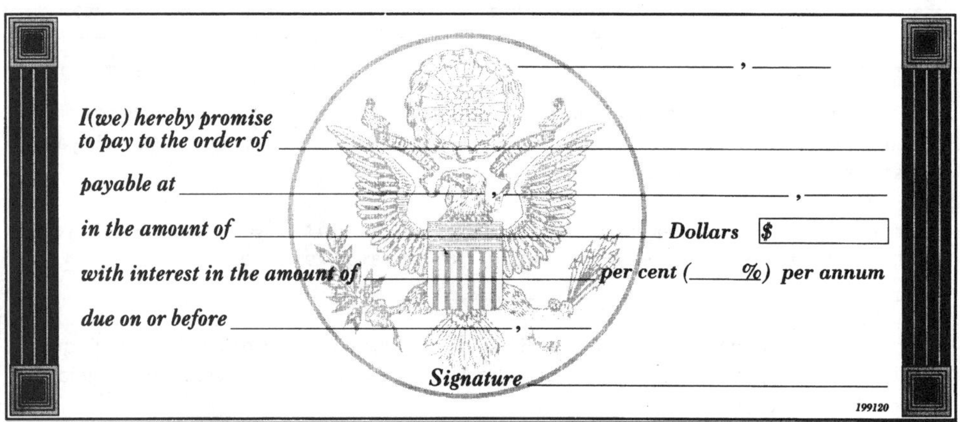

_______________, _______

I(we) hereby promise to pay to the order of _______________

payable at _______________, _______

in the amount of _______________ ***Dollars*** **$** _______

with interest in the amount of _______________ *per cent (_____%) per annum*

due on or before _______________, _______

Signature _______________

199120

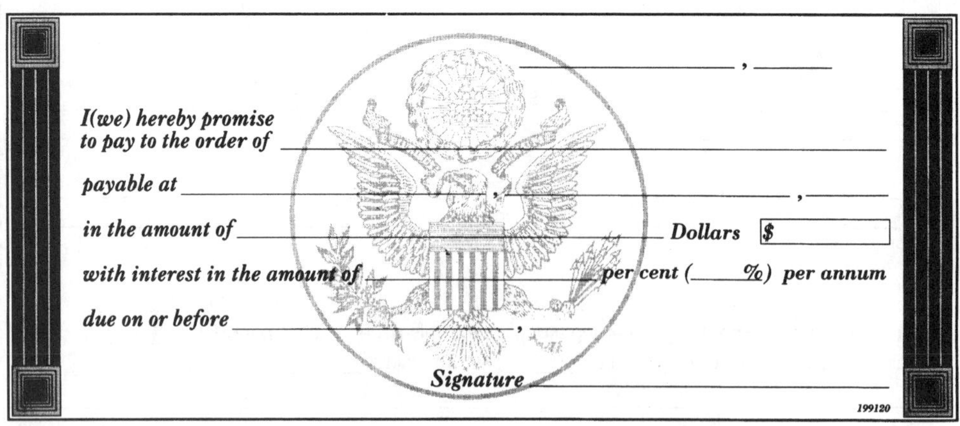

_______________, _______

I(we) hereby promise to pay to the order of _______________

payable at _______________, _______

in the amount of _______________ ***Dollars*** **$** _______

with interest in the amount of _______________ *per cent (_____%) per annum*

due on or before _______________, _______

Signature _______________

199120

GLOSSARY

Abstract of title A summary of the history of ownership of a property from public records. This history includes all changes of ownership and claims against the property.

Acceleration clause A provision in a loan document that makes the balance owed on a loan due and payable immediately after a specified event occurs. The event may be missing a payment or violating another provision of the loan.

Acknowledgment A formal declaration before a public official that one has signed a specific document.

Adjustable rate loan Adjustable rate mortgage, ARM; a loan that allows adjustments in the interest rate at specified times based on a named index.

Adjustable rate mortgage *See* Adjustable rate loan.

Adjusted sales price As a seller, the price for which you sell your home minus closing costs and commission, if applicable.

Agent A person authorized by another, the principal, to act for him or her in dealing with third parties.

AITD *See* All-inclusive trust deed.

Alienation clause *See* Due-on-sale clause.

All-inclusive trust deed Wraparound mortgage, AITD; a junior (second, third, and so forth) loan (mortgage or trust deed) at one overall interest rate used to wrap the existing loans into a package. The amount is sufficient to cover the existing loans and provide additional funds for the sellers. Sellers pay on existing loans from buyers' payments. Sellers remain primarily responsible for the original loans.

Amortization Gradual paying off of the principal on a loan by payment of regular installments of principal and interest.

Annual percentage rate APR; an interest rate that includes interest, discount points, origination fees, and loan broker's commission.

Appraisal An examination of a property by a qualified professional to estimate its market value as of a specific date.

APR *See* Annual percentage rate.

ARM *See* Adjustable rate loan.

Assessment Tax or charge by a governmental body for a specific public improvement covering the property owner's portion of costs. Assessments are in addition to normal property taxes.

Assign Transfer.

Assignee The person to whom interest is transferred.

Assignment Transfer of any property to another. Delegation of duties and rights to another.

Assignor The person from whom interest is transferred.

Assume Buyers taking over primary responsibility for payment of existing loan. Sellers then become secondarily liable for the loan and any deficiency judgment.

Assumption fee The fee a lender may charge for work involved in allowing buyers to assume primary liability for payment on an existing loan.

Attorney A person licensed to practice law by giving legal advice or assistance, as well as prosecuting and defending cases in courts.

Authorization to sell A listing contract allowing a real estate professional to act as an agent in the sale of property.

Bankruptcy Relief by a court of an obligation to pay money owed after turning over all property to a court-appointed trustee.

Basis The cost of a home when purchased, including down payment, loans, and closing costs.

Beneficiary The lender of money on a property used in a trust deed type of loan.

Beneficiary statement A statement provided by a lender using a trust deed type of loan that usually lists claims that do not appear on loan documents.

Bridge loan A short-term loan to buyers who are simultaneously selling one house and trying to buy another.

Broker *See* Real estate broker.

Buyer's agent A real estate broker or sales associate who represents the buyer in a transaction.

Buyer's broker A real estate broker who represents the buyer.

Buyer's market A condition in which there are more sellers than buyers; prices generally decrease.

Call Demand payment of a debt.

Capital asset Property, both real and personal, held by a taxpayer and not excluded by tax laws.

Capital gain Profit from selling or exchanging a capital asset in excess of the cost.

Capital improvements Additions to property that are permanent, increase property value, and have a useful life of more than one year.

Capital loss Loss from selling or exchanging property other than a personal residence at less than its cost.

Cashier's check A bank's own check guaranteed to be good by the bank at which it is drawn.

Casualty insurance *See* Hazard insurance.

CC&Rs Covenants, conditions, and restrictions; a document listing private restrictions on property. Often used when buyers have an interest in common areas.

Certificate of title A report, produced by a party providing abstracts of titles, stating that based on an examination of public records, the title is properly vested in the present owner.

Classified advertisements Advertisements that are separated by type and listed accordingly.

Closing Closing escrow, settlement; the final phase of a real estate transaction that involves signing loan documents, paying closing costs, and delivering the deed.

Closing costs Costs of sale; the additional expenses over and above the purchase price of buying and selling real estate.

Closing escrow *See* Closing.

Closing fee *See* Closing.

Closing statement A written, itemized account given to both seller and buyers at closing by the escrow holder and detailing receipts, disbursements, charges, credits, and prorations.

Commission Payments to an agent, such as a real estate broker, for services in the selling or buying of a home.

Commitment An oral or written agreement to make a loan made by a lender to a potential buyer.

Competent person A person who meets certain criteria set by a state for competency. These laws often include being a natural person who is an adult or an emancipated minor, mentally competent, and not a felon deprived of civil rights.

Conditions Requirements that must precede the performance or effectiveness of something else. Provisions or qualifications in a deed that if violated or not performed nullify the deed.

Condominium An undivided ownership in common in a portion of a piece of real property plus a separate interest in space in a building.

Consideration Anything of value that influences a person to enter into a contract, including money, a deed, an item of personal property, an act (including the payment of money), a service, or a promise (such as to pay on a loan). Acts or services must be performed *after* the seller and the buyers enter into the contract.

Contingency A condition on which a valid contract depends.

Contingency release Wipe-out clause, kick-out provision; provisions providing that the sellers will continue to market their home until they receive another offer to purchase their home that does not contain the contingencies the sellers indicated or buyers remove those contingencies the sellers specified. After the sellers receive a contract without the detailed contingencies, the original buyers have the specified time agreed on to remove the contingencies or the sellers may sell their home to the buyers who offered them a contract without the contingencies.

Contract for deed *See* Land sales contract.

Controller's deed *See* Tax deed.

Conventional loan A loan that is not guaranteed or insured by a government agency.

Convey Transfer.

Costs of sale *See* Closing costs.

Counteroffer A statement by a person to whom an offer is made proposing a new offer to the original offeror.

Covenants Agreements or promises contained in and conveyed by a deed that are inseparable from the property. Pledges or the performance or nonperformance of certain acts or the use or nonuse of property.

Cram down *See* Short Sale.

Credit report A detailed report of a person's credit history and rating.

Deed A document containing a detailed written description of the property that transfers property ownership.

Deed of trust *See* Trust deed.

Default Failure of a person to fulfill an obligation or perform a duty; failure to make a loan payment when it is due.

Deficiency judgment A court decision making an individual personally liable for payoff of a remaining amount due because the full amount was not obtained by foreclosure.

Delinquent payment A payment that was not paid when it was due.

Demand fee Demand for payoff charge; a fee for a written request to a lender for lender's demand for payment of the loan in full and the supporting documents necessary for release of the lien against the property.

Deposit Money that buyers submit with a purchase offer as evidence of their intention and ability to buy.

Depreciation Loss in value from any cause.

Disclosure Making known things that were previously unknown.

Discount points *See* Points.

Discovery Disclosure of things previously unknown.

Divided agency Agent's action in representing both parties in a transaction without the knowledge and consent of both.

Down payment Money that the sellers and buyers agree on, or that a lender requires, that buyers pay toward the purchase price before escrow can close.

Dual agent A broker acting either directly or through an associate licensee as agent for both seller and buyer.

Due-on-sale clause Alienation clause; an acceleration clause in a loan giving the lender the right to demand all sums owed due at once and payable if the property owner transfers title.

Earnest money *See* Deposit.

Emancipated minor A person who is under the age to legally be an adult in the state in which they live but who has some other criteria that allow them to function as adults. The criteria may include being lawfully married or divorced, duty in the armed forces, or emancipated by court order.

Eminent domain Governments' power that allows them to take private property for public use after paying what they feel to be a fair price.

Encumbrance A charge, claim, or lien against a property or personal right or interest in a property that affects or limits the title but does not prevent transfer.

Equity The part of a property's current value that is owned and on which no money is owed; the property's value minus the liens owed against the property.

Escrow A process in the transfer of real property in which buyers and sellers deposit documents or money with a neutral third party (the escrow holder). Buyers and sellers give instructions to the escrow holder to hold and deliver documents and money if certain conditions are met.

Escrow instructions A written agreement between seller and buyers that extrapolates the purchase contract into a form used as directions on how to conduct and close the escrow.

Exclusive agency listing A listing with only one agency that provides that if the real estate professional obtains the buyer, the seller must pay the broker the commission. If you sell your home yourself, you are not liable for the commission.

Exclusive right to sell listing A listing providing that during the time listed only that broker has the right to sell your home and earn the commission, no matter who makes the sale.

Extended coverage title insurance This coverage protects against numerous risks that are not a matter of record.

FHA Federal Housing Administration; a federal governmental agency that manages FHA-insured loans to protect lenders in case of default by buyers.

FHA loan Financing by having a conventional loan made by a lender and insured by the FHA.

Fiduciary A person who is in a position of trust who must act in the best interest of clients.

Fire insurance *See* Hazard insurance.

Fixed-rate loan A loan on which the percentage of interest remains at the same rate over the life of the loan. The payments of principal remain equal during the entire period.

Fixture Items permanently attached to or for which special openings were made in a home and its associated structures.

Fix-up costs The expenses of improvements, repairs, and attractiveness items.

Foreclosure The process by which a property on which a borrower has not paid is sold to satisfy a loan against the property.

Fraud Willfully concealing or misrepresenting a material fact to influence another person to take action. The action results in the person's loss of property or legal rights.

FSBO For sale by owner; a phrase describing a homeowner selling property without using a real estate broker.

Gift deed A deed given for love and affection.

Grant deed A deed using the word *grant* in the clause that transfers ownership.

Grantee Buyer; receiver of a title to a property.

Grantor Seller; holder of a title to a property.

Guarantee of title A warranty that title is vested in the party shown on the deed.

Hazard insurance Casualty insurance, fire insurance; insurance protection against stated specific hazards, such as fire, hail, windstorms, earthquakes, floods, civil disturbances, explosions, riots, theft, and vandalism.

Home equity line of credit Credit given by a lender based on the amount of one's equity in a property. The line of credit becomes a loan secured by a mortgage or trust deed when the borrower uses some or all of the credit.

Home inspection *See* Physical inspection.

Home inspector A qualified person who examines and reports on the general condition of a home's site and structures.

Homeowner association dues Monthly fees owners of homes pay to their homeowner association for the items it provides.

Homeowner's insurance A policy protecting a homeowner from liability and casualty hazards listed in the policy.

Impounds Reserve fund; funds held by the lender to ensure payment in the future of recurring expenses. These expenses can include insurance premiums and taxes.

Improper delivery Delivery of a deed that has not passed out of seller's control and/or was not delivered to buyers during the seller's lifetime.

Improvement costs Expenses for permanent additions.

Imputed interest rate The minimum rate the IRS requires for a seller-financed loan. If the seller charges less than the minimum rate, the IRS taxes the seller on the minimum.

Index A measurement of interest rates on which changes in interest charges on adjustable rate loans are based.

Inspection records Notices indicating that inspections have been conducted by the proper local authorities at certain specified points in the building process.

Inspection reports Reports by inspectors about the condition of various aspects of your property, including defects and repairs considered necessary.

Installment note A loan paid back in at least two payments of principal on different dates.

Installment sale A sale that allows the seller to receive payments in more than one tax year.

Interest A charge or rate paid in arrears (after incurred) to a lender for borrowing money.

Interest-only loan A loan for which only the interest is paid and no principal is repaid until the final installment.

Jointly and severally liable Liable along with other parties and personally liable.

Joint tenancy Vesting wherein two or more parties acquire title at the same time. Each party has an equal, undivided interest and equal right to possess the property, including automatic right of survivorship.

Judgment Final determination by a court of a matter presented to it. A general monetary obligation on all property of the person who owes the money. This obligation applies in each county where an abstract of the court judgment was recorded.

Lack of capacity Inability to enter into a contract because one is not a competent person by his or her state's criteria.

Landlord The owner or lessor of real property.

Land sales contract Contract for deed, real property sales contract; an agreement in which the seller retains title to property until the buyer performs all contract conditions.

Lease A contract that transfers possession and use of designated property for a limited, stated time under specified conditions.

Lease option A contract that stipulates that potential buyers are leasing a property for an agreed-on rental payment. These buyers have the right to purchase the property before the specified future date for the amount listed in the contract. Part of the lease payment is considered option money toward the purchase price.

Lease purchase A contract that states that buyers are leasing the property for the agreed-on amount and conditions. The buyers agree to purchase the property at the agreed-on time for the agreed-on amount.

Legal description A formal description giving a property's location, size, and boundaries in written and/or map form.

Lessee The tenant or person who leases property from the landlord to use it.

Lessor The landlord or owner of property who leases the property to the tenant for the tenant's use.

Liability Responsibility for damages to other people or property; what you owe against an asset.

Lien A claim against a property making the property security for debts, such as loans, mechanic's liens, and taxes.

Lien releases Documents releasing one from monetary liability to the party listed after fully paying that party.

Liquidated damages The amount of money the seller may keep if the buyers default or breach the contact.

Lis pendens An official recorded notice that legal action is pending against the title to the property.

Listing Authorization to sell; a contract allowing a real estate broker to act as an agent to buy, lease, or sell property for another.

Loan disclosure statement A lender's account summary required by the Federal Truth in Lending Act.

Loan discount fee *See* Points.

Loan fees One-time charges by the lender for initiating a loan, including points, appraisal, and credit report on buyers.

Loan origination fee Lender's charge for arranging and processing a loan, usually based on a percentage of the loan.

Loan tie-in fee A fee charged by whoever handles closing for their work and liability in conforming to the lender's criteria for the buyers' new loan.

Market value The amount buyers are willing to pay and sellers are willing to accept within a reasonable time.

Marshal's deed *See* Sheriff's deed.

Mechanic's lien A claim filed against property by a contractor, service provider, or supplier for work done or materials provided for which full payment has not been received.

MLS *See* Multiple Listing Service.

Mortgage A contract to secure a loan by which the seller promises his or her property without giving up possession or title.

Mortgage default insurance Default insurance; insurance coverage enabling the lender to receive a part of the outstanding balance in the event the owner defaults.

Mortgagee Lender of money on property using a mortgage.

Mortgagor Property owner who borrows money using a mortgage.

Multiple Listing Service MLS; an agency to which real estate brokers belong to pool their listings with other brokers. If a sale is made, the listing and selling brokers share the commission.

Negative amortization Process in which payments on a loan do not cover interest payments and the difference between the payment and interest due are added to the loan balance.

Net listing A listing providing that the broker retain all money received in excess of the price set by the seller.

Nominal interest rate Interest rate stated in a promissory note.

Notary fee A charge paid to a notary public to witness signatures on some of the legal documents in a transaction.

Notice of default Warning sent to a borrower on a loan cautioning the borrower that the payment is delinquent.

Offset statement A statement regarding a loan provided by the seller when a beneficiary statement is not available.

Open listing A nonexclusive right-to-sell agreement one can make with one or more real estate professionals. It provides that if you sell your home yourself, you are not liable to the broker for a commission. If, however, a real estate professional obtains the buyers for the property, you must pay the broker the commission you have negotiated.

Option A contract to keep an offer to buy, sell, or lease property open for a period and under the terms agreed on.

Optionee The person who gets the option on a property.

Optionor The owner of a title who gives an option.

Option to buy *See* Purchase option.

Payment records Checks, receipts, and written ledgers.

Payment statements Monthly stubs showing your payment date, amounts applied to principal and interest, and remaining balance due, as well as annual summary statements.

Permission-to-show listing A listing contract that allows a real estate professional to show a seller's property only to the person or persons named in that contract. You pay the commission only if someone on the list purchases the seller's home.

Personal property Items that are not permanently attached to your home or other structures on your property.

Pest control inspection Structural pest control inspection, termite inspection; inspection for infestation or infection by wood-destroying pests or organisms.

Physical inspection Home inspection; examination of the general physical condition of a property's site and structures.

Planned unit development PUD; a subdivision in which the lots are separately owned but other areas are owned in common.

Points Discount points, loan discount fee; a one-time charge by the lender to adjust the yield on the loan to current market conditions or to adjust the rate on the loan to market rate. Each point is equal to 1 percent of the loan balance.

Power of attorney A document that gives one person the power to sign documents for another person.

Power of sale clause A provision in a loan allowing the lender to foreclose and sell borrower's property publicly without a court procedure.

Preliminary title report Report summarizing the title search performed by a title company or lawyer for a property.

Prepayment penalty A fine imposed on a borrower by a lender for the early payoff of a loan or any substantial part of a loan.

Principal One of the parties in a real estate transaction, either the seller or the buyers. In a loan, the amount of money borrowed.

Principal residence An IRS term denoting the residence wherein you spend the most time during the tax year.

Probate court A court that handles wills and the administration of estates of people who have died.

Promissory note The written contract you sign promising to pay a definite amount of money by a definite future date.

Property taxes Taxes assessed on property at a uniform rate so that the amount of the tax depends on the value.

Property tax statements Documents that the county assessor's office mails to homeowners itemizing the semiannual or annual tax bill on a home and indicating the payment due dates.

Prorations Proportional distributions of responsibility for the payment of the expenses of homeownership. This distribution is based on the percentage of an assessment or billing period during which the seller and buyers own the property.

Purchase contract The contract containing terms and conditions to which the seller and the buyers agree when the seller accepts the offer to purchase their home.

Purchase option Option to buy; the type of contract in which buyers agree to purchase the property for the amount listed in the contract, if they decide to buy the seller's home and make the purchase within the listed period of time, and agree that the seller keeps the option fee if they do not buy the property.

Quitclaim deed A deed using the word *quitclaim* in the clause granting ownership and thus releasing the grantor from any claim to that property. A quitclaim deed has no warranties.

Real estate *See* Real property.

Real estate broker A real estate agent who represents another person in dealing with third parties. This person must take required courses, pass a broker's exam, and be licensed by the state. A broker may employ other qualified individuals and is responsible for their actions.

Real estate professional A real estate broker or sales associate.

Real estate sales agent A person who is licensed by a state and who represents a real estate broker in transactions.

Real Estate Settlement Procedures Act *See* RESPA.

Real property Real estate; land and whatever is built on, growing on, or attached to the land.

Real property sales contract *See* Land sales contract.

Reconveyance deed A deed that records full satisfaction of a trust deed-secured debt on your property and transfers bare legal title from the trustee to you.

Recording Official entry of liens, reconveyances, and transactions into the permanent records of a county.

Release of contract An agreement that all responsibilities and rights occurring as a result of a contract are invalid.

Repair costs Expenses for work maintaining a home's condition, including replacement and restoration.

Request for notice of default A recorded notice allowing a county recorder to notify lenders of foreclosure on a property in which the lender has an interest.

Rescind To cancel a contract and restore the parties to the state they would have been in had the contract never been made.

RESPA Real Estate Settlement Procedures Act; a federal law that requires that buyers be given, in advance of closing, information regarding their loan.

Revocation Involuntary cancellation that occurs when the time limit has expired *and* one or both parties do not perform in accordance with the terms of the contract.

Sales associate A real estate professional with either a broker's or sales license who acts as an agent for a broker.

Sale leaseback An agreement in which the seller sells the property to buyers who agree to lease the property back to the seller.

Satisfaction of mortgage A document indicating that the owner has paid their mortgage off in full.

Seller buy-down loan A loan in which the effective interest rate is bought down (reduced) during the beginning years of the loan by contributions a seller makes.

Seller carry-back loan A loan for which the seller acts as a lender to carry back or hold mortgage notes from buyers. These notes may be first, second, or even third loans.

Seller's agent *See* Listing.

Seller's market A condition in which there are more buyers than sellers; prices generally increase.

Selling agent *See* Buyer's agent.

Settlement *See* Closing.

Severalty Vesting of title in which you hold title by yourself.

Sheriff's deed Marshal's deed; a deed used by courts in foreclosure or in carrying out a judgment. This deed transfers a debtor's title to a buyer.

Short sale A lender selling a property for less than the amount of the loan.

Single agent An agent representing only one party in a real estate transaction.

Specific performance Law that allows one party to sue another to perform as specified under the terms of their contract.

Standard-coverage title insurance The regular investigation for this insurance generally reveals only matters of record and location of the improvements with respect to the lot line.

Straight note A promise to pay a loan in which the principal is paid as one lump sum, although the interest may be paid in one lump sum or in installments.

Subject-to loan An existing loan for which buyers take over responsibility for the payments, and seller remains primarily liable in the event of a deficiency judgment.

Take sheet A form used to collect information necessary to prepare the escrow instructions.

Tax deed Controller's deed; a deed used by a state to transfer title to the buyers.

Taxes *See* Property taxes.

Tax stamps A method of denoting that a transfer tax has been paid in which stamps are affixed to a deed before the deed may be recorded.

Termination of agency Ending of an agency agreement.

Time is of the essence A statement that one party in a contract must perform certain acts within the stated period before the other party can perform.

Title Evidence of one's right to a property and the extent of that right.

Title insurance The policy issued to you by the title company on completion of the final title search protecting against claims in the future based on circumstances in the past.

Title insurance companies Companies issuing title insurance policies.

Title search An examination of information recorded on the seller's property at the county recorder's office. This examination verifies that the property has no outstanding claims or liens against it to adversely affect the buyer or lender and that the seller can transfer clear legal title to the property.

Transfer fee *See* Assumption fee.

Transfer tax Documentary transfer tax; a tax that some states allow individual counties or cities to place on the transferring of real property.

Trust deed A document, used as a security device for the loan on your property, by which you transfer bare (naked) legal title with the power of sale to a trustee. This transfer is in effect until you have totally paid off the loan.

Trustee A person who holds bare legal title to a property without being the actual owner of the property. The trustee has the power of sale for the lender's benefit.

Trustee's deed A deed used by a trustee in a foreclosure handled outside of court to transfer the debtor's title to buyers.

Trust funds Funds held by a closing agent or escrow holder for the benefit of the buyers or seller.

Truth in lending A federal law that requires disclosure of loan terms to a borrower who is using his or her principal residence as security for a loan.

Unconditional lien release Waiver of liens; a release, usually signed by a contractor, after a job is complete and you made the final payments waiving and releasing all rights and claims against your home.

Unenforceable Not able to be enforced; void.

Unlawful detainer The unjustifiable keeping of possession of real property by someone who originally had the right to possession but no longer has that right.

Usury Interest charged in excess of what state law permits.

VA Veterans Administration; the federal government agency that manages VA loans.

VA loan GI loan; financing made by having a conventional loan made by a lender guaranteed by the VA.

Vendee Purchaser or buyer.

Vendor Owner or seller.

Vesting Interest that cannot be revoked.

Veterans Administration *See* VA.

Void To have no effect; not enforceable by law.

Voidable Able to be set aside.

Waive Unilateral voluntary relinquishment of a right of which one is aware.

Walk-through inspection Buyers' physical examination of a property within a few days before closing, verifying that systems, appliances, and the house itself are in the agreed-on condition.

Warranties Printed or written documents guaranteeing the condition of property or its components.

Warranty deed A deed in which the grantor explicitly guarantees the title to be as indicated in the deed. The grantor agrees to protect buyers against all claimants to the property.

Wrap-around mortgage *See* All-inclusive trust deed.

Zoning Governmental laws establishing building codes and governing the specific uses of land and buildings.

INDEX

Main entries are boldfaced for your convenience.